AF693728

NAVIGATING YOUR FINANCES GOD'S WAY

FACILITATORS GUIDE
Small Group Study

© 2011 Compass—*finances God's way*TM
All Rights Reserved
Revisions and Crisis Chapter © 2011 Howard L. Dayton, Jr.
All Rights Reserved
217 N. Westmonte Drive, Suite 2014
Altamonte Springs, Flordia 32714
February 2014 edition

www.compass1.org

American Bible Society helped fund the production of *Navigating Your Finances*.
We are grateful to serve together to encourage meaningful Bible engagement.

This publication is designed to provide accurate and authoritative information with regard to the subject matter covered. It is sold with the understanding that the publisher is not engaged in rendering legal, accounting, or other professional advice. If legal advice or other expert professional assistance is required, the services of a competent professional person should be sought. –From a Declaration of Principles jointly adopted by a Committee of the American Bar Association and a Committee of Publishers and Associations.

Published by Compass—*finances God's way*™

Verses identified as (KJV) are taken from the King James Version.

Verses identified as (NIV) are taken from the Holy Bible: New International Version, © 1973, 1978, 1984 by the International Bible Society. Used by permission of Zondervan Bible Publishers.

Verses identified as (TLB) are taken from The Living Bible, © 1971 by Tyndale House Publishers, Wheaton, Il. Used by permission.

All other verses are taken from the New American Standard Bible, © 1960,1962, 1963, 1968, 1971, 1973, 1975, 1977, 1995 by the Lockman Foundation. Used by permission.

WELCOME!

I am so thankful that you have decided to facilitate the *Navigating Your Finances* small group study. The Lord has used the principles you are about to learn in the lives of millions of people around the world. We've learned that people benefit most when they are faithful to complete the following.

First of all, before the group meets, read *Your Money Counts*. This book is easy to read and will provide you with a good overview of the study.

Then, complete these before each weekly meeting.

1. **Homework Questions.** The homework questions will take only about 15 minutes each day to complete. Space is provided in the Workbook to answer the questions. If a married couple takes the study, each will use a separate Workbook.

2. **Scripture Memory.** Memorize an assigned verse from the Bible each week and individually recite the verse at the beginning of class. This will help you remember the most important principles.

3. **Let's Get Practical!** Complete a practical financial exercise, such as beginning a spending plan or designing a debt repayment plan.

4. **Prayer.** Everyone prays for the other group members each day. Answers to prayers are one of the most encouraging parts of the small group experience.

If an individual is unable to complete the requirements for a particular week, we recommend that he or she refrain from participating in the class discussion. This accountability helps us to be faithful. And the more faithful we are, the more benefits we receive from the study.

Attendance. Everyone should attend at least 7 of the 9 weekly meetings. Please ask the participants to notify you in advance if they anticipate missing a meeting or arriving late.

Again, we are very grateful that you have decided to facilitate the *Navigating Your Finances* study. I pray that the Lord will bless you in every way as you help others learn and practice His way of handling money.

Howard Dayton

Howard Dayton
Founder, Compass—*finances God's way*™

INFORMATION LEADERS NEED TO KNOW

SMALL GROUP STUDY SCHEDULE

WEEK	CHAPTER	PAGE	LET'S GET PRACTICAL!
1	Introduction	7	Read *Your Money Counts*
2	God's Part & Our Part	15	Deed, List of Assets, Begin 30 Day Tracking Income & Spending
3	Debt	49	Debt List & Snowball 'Em!, Compass—*finances God's way* Map™, Continue 30 Day Tracking Income & Spending
4	Honesty & Counsel	81	Life Insurance Needs, Filing, Continue 30 Day Tracking Income & Spending
5	Generosity	109	Journey of Generosity, Continue 30 Day Tracking Income & Spending
6	Work	129	Personality Assessment and Estimated Spending Plan
7	Saving & Investing	157	Begin Tracking Spending Plan, Tweak Spending Plan, Net Worth Calculation
8	Crisis & Perspective	189	Estate preparation, Continue Tracking & Tweaking Spending Plan
9	Eternity	233	Life Goals, Continue Tracking & Tweaking Spending Plan
	Prayer Logs	262	
	Care Logs	274	

1

INTRODUCTION

FACILITATORS GUIDE

"If therefore you have not been faithful in the use of worldly wealth, who will entrust the true riches to you?" (Luke 16:11).

INTRODUCTION

Facilitators Guide for Week 1

Overview

The primary objectives for week 1 are to begin to develop close relationships among the participants and to review the study requirements.

Note: The blank space following each agenda number is for the facilitator to fill in the scheduled time for each agenda item. For example, if your class begins at 7:00, #1 would read 7:00, #2 would read 7:05, and so forth. This is designed to help you monitor the time so that the class will end punctually.

Agenda

1. __________ (5 minutes) Open in prayer.

2. __________ (5 minutes) Each person individually recites from memory:

"If therefore you have not been faithful in the use of worldly wealth, who will entrust the true riches to you?" (Luke 16:11).

3. ___________ (70 minutes) Ask each person to introduce themselves, beginning with a facilitator. Ask them to share how they were introduced to Jesus Christ, what they do for a living, and something about their family. To determine how much time each person is allotted, divide the number of people into 70 minutes. If a participant is too brief, gently ask additional questions to provide an opportunity to express himself or herself more fully.

4. __________ (15 minutes) Begin the **homework** discussion.

Homework Questions

1. What was the most helpful information you learned from reading *Your Money Counts*?

2. What are two practical principles from the book you can apply now?

Read Isaiah 55:8-9.

3. Based on this passage, do you think God's way of handling money will differ from how most people handle it? What do you think would be the greatest differences?

Note: Compass' comments, bracketed in parenthesis, will follow each question. Following the comments there will be a space for the facilitator's answers.

[God's economy operates on totally different principles. The biggest difference is most people don't believe the Lord plays a role in finances, but the Bible reveals He has the dominant role.]

4. What benefits do you hope to receive from participating in this study?

5. What are your personal goals concerning your:

Income—

Giving—

Saving—

Getting out of Debt—

Read the Introduction Notes on pages 11-13, you may download a free MP3 version of the notes to listen to. These can be found by going to www.compass1.org, clicking on Small Group Studies Tools & Resources and then clicking on the Navigating Study *Student and Facilitator Tools*.

6. What information especially interested you and why did it interest you?

[Emphasize that how we handle money affects our fellowship with Christ.]

7. When you learned the three reasons the Bible says so much about money, how did this challenge your thinking?

Remaining Agenda

1. ___________ (5 minutes) Play the Week 1 segment of the *Navigating Your Finances* DVD
2. ___________ (5 minutes) Review what the participants are to do for the next class.
   - ☐ Complete the **Homework** on pages 16-24.
   - ☐ Complete the **List Your Assets** on pages 35-36.
   - ☐ Complete the **Deed** on pages 37-39.
   - ☐ Begin recording your **Income & Spending** on pages 40-47.
   - ☐ Remind everyone to begin memorizing 1 Chronicles 29:11-12 now because of its length, and remind them to do the homework daily.
   - ☐ Review the calendar to determine if any regularly scheduled classes fall on a holiday. If there are conflicts, please reschedule.
   - ☐ Schedule the social.
   - ☐ Complete the Prayer Logs. There should be one Prayer Log for each person or couple.
3. ___________ (10 minutes) Take prayer requests and note them in the Prayer Log.
4. ___________ (5 minutes) End in prayer.

INTRODUCTION NOTES

Please read notes *after* completing Homework question 5.

This study will transform your life and finances as you learn what the God of the universe says about handling money. This study is for everyone—single or married, young or old, whether you earn a lot or a little.

The way most people handle money stands in sharp contrast to God's financial principles. Isaiah 55:8 puts it like this: *"For my thoughts are not your thoughts, neither are your ways my ways,' declares the Lord"* (NIV). The most significant difference between the two is the Bible reveals God is closely involved with our finances. Many people fail to realize it because He has chosen to be invisible to us and to operate in the unseen supernatural realm.

THE BIBLE AND MONEY

It may surprise you to learn how much the Bible has to say about finances. More than 2,350 verses address God's way of handling money and possessions. What's more, fifteen percent of everything Jesus Christ said has to do with money—how we view it and how we handle it. And He made such a major point of teaching these things for three reasons:

1. How we handle money impacts our fellowship with the Lord.

We may think we can separate our spiritual lives and our financial lives into two different compartments. Not so! Over and over, Jesus equates how we handle our money with the quality of our spiritual life. In Luke 16:11, He says, *"Therefore if you have not been faithful in the use of worldly* wealth, who will entrust the true riches to you?"* The true riches in life grow out of a close relationship with the Lord.

It's a simple fact: If we handle money according to the principles of Scripture, we *will* enjoy closer fellowship with Christ. The parable of the talents demonstrates this, as the master congratulates the servant who managed his money faithfully: *"Well done, good and faithful* [servant]. *You were faithful with a few things, I will put you in charge of many things;* ***enter into the joy of your master****"* (Matthew 25:21, emphasis added). We can enter into the joy of a more intimate relationship with the Lord as we handle money His way.

2. Money and possessions compete with God for first place in our lives.

We may never say it in so many words, but money is often a primary competitor with Christ for our affection. Jesus tells us we must choose to serve only one of these two masters. *"No one can serve two masters. Either he will hate the one and love the other, or he will be devoted to the one and despise the other. You cannot serve both God and money"* (Matthew 6:24, NIV). We *use* money, yes, but it's impossible for us to *serve* money and still serve and love the Lord.

During the Crusades of the 12th Century, the Crusaders hired mercenaries to fight for them. Because it was a religious war, the mercenaries were baptized before fighting. Before going under the water, however, the soldiers would take their swords and hold them up out of the water to symbolize that Jesus Christ was *not* in control of their weapons. They claimed freedom to use their weapons in any way they wished.

Unfortunately, that illustrates the way many people today handle their money as they hold their wallet or purse "out of the water." Their attitude is, "God, you may be Lord of my entire life—except in the area of money. I'm perfectly capable of handling that myself."

3. God wants us to be money smart.

The Lord also talked so much about money because He knew that from time to time money problems would be a challenge for all of us. Stress and confusion in this area of life can impact our marriage, our family life, our happiness, and even our health. Because He loves and cares for us so deeply, He wanted to equip us to make the wisest possible financial decisions.

A DIVISION OF RESPONSIBILITIES

Years ago, my close friend Jim Seneff asked me to join him in a study of the Bible to discover what the Lord said about money. Carefully reading through the pages of Scripture, we identified 2,350 verses related to money and possessions. As we arranged these passages topic by topic, we were amazed by how *practical* they were. In the process, we discovered an important pattern—or, what you might call a division of responsibilities in the handling of money.

Simply put, God has a role, and we have a role. As you progress through this study, you may be surprised to learn which responsibilities are God's, and which are yours.

You will also discover that learning and applying God's way of handling money is a marathon, rather than a sprint. In fact, gaining financial wisdom is a lifelong journey. When we learn God's responsibilities and our own, we will experience contentment, hope, and confidence about our financial future. Let the journey begin!

FEATURES

Compass—*finances God's way map*™

We have developed the map to help you on your journey to *financial faithfulness.* The map enables you to identify where you are, where you want to be and your next step to take for financial progress.

Recommended Resources
At the end of most lessons, we recommend outstanding books, Web sites, financial tools and calculators, and organizations that will help you on your journey.

www.compass1.org
The Compass web site is a dynamic site created to accompany this study. It contains online tools, videos, and answers to frequently asked questions.

Allow me to add this one personal note: As I wrote this study, I prayed for you. I truly did. No, I may never have the privilege of meeting you personally, but I prayed that each and every person who embarks on this journey would experience the tremendous sense of hope, peace, and encouragement that comes from discovering God's way of handling money. I am excited even as I write these words, because I know that great things are in store for you.

2

GOD'S PART & OUR PART

FACILITATORS GUIDE

"Everything in the heavens and earth is yours, O Lord, and this is your kingdom. We adore you as being in control of everything. Riches and honor come from you alone, and you are the Ruler of all mankind; your hand controls power and might and it is at your discretion that men are made great and given strength"
(1 Chronicles 29:11-12, TLB).

GOD'S PART & OUR PART

Facilitators Guide for Week 2

Overview

This is the most important section because the remainder of the study builds on understanding God's ownership of everything.

Let's Get Practical!

☐ Complete **List Your Assets** on pages 35-36.

☐ Complete the **Deed** on pages 37-39.

☐ Read **Budget Options** on page 40 and select the type of budget you prefer to use.

☐ Begin recording your **Income & Spending** on pages 44-45.

Agenda

1. __________ (5 minutes) Open in prayer.

2. __________ (5 minutes) Each person individually recites from memory:

"Everything in the heavens and earth is yours, O Lord, and this is your kingdom. We adore you as being in control of everything. Riches and honor come from you alone, and you are the Ruler of all mankind; your hand controls power and might, and it is at your discretion that men are made great and given strength"
(1 Chronicles 29:11-12, TLB).

3. __________ (85 minutes) Begin the group discussion.

Reminder: The discussion for *each day's* homework proceeds as follows: (1) Assign one passage of Scripture from that day's homework to each person to read (as far as the verses will go); (2) Proceed in a circle, asking each person to answer *all* the questions for that day's homework. If the answer to a question is obvious, it's unnecessary for more than one person to answer the question. If you're running out of time, ask the responses to be brief.

Day One (God's ownership)

Complete List Your Assets and the Deed and begin keeping a record of everything you spend.

1. Do you have any questions about these?

2. What did you learn from completing them? How do you think this will influence you in the future?

Read *Deuteronomy 10:14; Psalm 24:1* and *1 Corinthians 10:26.*

3. What do these passages say about the ownership of your possessions? What do you own?

[The Lord owns everything in the world.]

Read *Leviticus 25:23; Psalm 50:10-12* and *Haggai 2:8.*

4. What are some of the items that the Lord owns?

Leviticus 25:23— [God owns all the land.]

Psalm 50:10-12— [God owns all the animals.]

Haggai 2:8— [God owns all the gold and silver.]

5. Evaluate your attitude toward your possessions. Do you consistently recognize the true owner? What are two practical suggestions to help you recognize God's ownership?

[Consider altering your vocabulary by dropping the possessive pronouns ("my", "mine", and "ours") and substituting "His" or "the" instead. For thirty days, each morning and night, meditate and prayerfully recite *1 Chronicles 29:11-12.*]

Day Two (God's Control)

Read *1 Chronicles 29:11-12* and *Psalm 135:6.*

1. What do these passages say about the Lord's control of circumstances?

[The Lord is in control of all circumstances.]

Read *Proverbs 21:1; Isaiah 40:21-24* and *Acts 17:26.*

2. What do these verses tell you about the Lord's control of people?

Proverbs 21:1— [God controls the heart of each person.]

Isaiah 40:21-24— [The Lord completely controls all people.]

Acts 17:26— [The Lord controls the boundaries and duration of every nation].

3. Do you normally recognize the Lord's control of all events? If not, how can you become more consistent?

Day Three (Challenging circumstances)

Read *Genesis 45:4-8* and *Romans 8:28.*

1. Why is it important to realize that God controls and uses even difficult circumstances for good in the life of a godly person?

[God uses all circumstances for good in the lives of those who love and obey Him. Joseph suffered difficulties, but God orchestrated them for ultimate good.]

2. How does this perspective impact you?

3. Share a difficult circumstance you have experienced and how the Lord used it for good in your life.

* *Facilitator,* you should have approximately **one hour** of class time remaining.

Day Four (God's Provision)

Read *Psalm 34:9-10; Matthew 6:31-33* and *Philippians 4:19.*

1. What has the Lord promised concerning meeting your needs?

[God promises to meet our needs if we put Him first in our lives and seek His righteousness.]

2. How does this promise apply to you now?

3. Give an example from the Bible of the Lord providing for someone's needs in a supernatural way.

[Several of the many examples of God's provision: Israel in the wilderness (Exodus 16:4-35), Jesus feeding the five thousand (Matthew 14:15-21) and the four thousand (Matthew 15:32-38), and the Lord sending ravens to feed Elijah (1 Kings 17:4-6).]

Day Five (Our Role)

Read *1 Corinthians 4:2.*

1. According to this verse what is your requirement as a steward and how would you define a steward?

[We are responsible to be faithful stewards. A steward is a manager of another's property.]

Read *Luke 16:1-2.*

2. Why did the master remove the steward from his position and how does that apply to you?

[The steward was removed because he squandered his master's possessions. If we squander the possessions the Lord entrusts to us, we can expect the same.]

Read *Luke 16:10.*

3. Describe the principle found in this verse.

[If a person is unfaithful in a little matter, he or she will be unfaithful with much. The reverse is also true. It is important to be faithful in small matters.]

4. How does this apply in your situation?

Day Six (the Notes)

Read the God's Part & Our Part Notes on pages 25-34.

1. What did you learn that was especially helpful?

2. How will you apply it?

3. I will take the following *action* as a result of this week's study:

Remaining Agenda

1. __________ (10 minutes) Play the Week 2 segment of the *Navigating Your Finances* DVD.

2. __________ (10 minutes) Note in the Prayer Log requests and answers to prayers.

3. __________ (5 minutes) End in prayer.

Reminder for Facilitators: Contact each participant this week and record it in the Care Log on page 274 or 275.

GOD'S PART & OUR PART NOTES

Please read *after* completing Day 5 homework.

This is the most important section of the entire study. Why? *Because how we view God determines how we live.* In the Bible God calls Himself by more than 250 names. The name that best describes God's part in the area of money is *Lord.*

After losing his children and all his possessions—in a single day!—Job continued to worship God. Even in his grief, he understood God's role as Lord of those possessions. Moses walked away from the treasures of Egypt, choosing instead to suffer with God's people, because he accepted God's role as Lord of all. There are three elements to God's role: ownership, control, and provision.

OWNERSHIP

The Lord owns all our possessions. *"To the LORD your God belong...the earth and everything in it"* (Deuteronomy 10:14, NIV). *"The earth is the LORD's, and all it contains"* (Psalm 24:1).

Scripture even reveals specific items God owns. Leviticus 25:23 identifies Him as the owner of all the land: *"The land...shall not be sold permanently, for the land is Mine."* Haggai 2:8 says that He owns the precious metals: *"'The silver is Mine and the gold is Mine,' declares the LORD of hosts."* And in Psalm 50 we are told that God owns the animals. *"Every beast of the forest is Mine, the cattle on a thousand hills...everything that moves in the field is Mine. If I were hungry, I would not tell you, for the world is Mine, and all it contains"* (Psalm 50:10-12). And in 2 Corinthians 1:21-22 the Bible declares the Lord owns us: *"...He* [God] *anointed us, set his seal of ownership on us, and put his Spirit in our hearts...."*

The Lord created all things, and He never transferred the ownership of His creation to people. You and I own nothing! Zero! Absolutely nothing! As we will see throughout this study, recognizing God's ownership is crucial in allowing Jesus Christ to become the Lord of our money and possessions.

OUR OWNERSHIP OR HIS LORDSHIP?

If we are to be genuine followers of Christ, we must transfer ownership of our possessions to the Lord. *"None of you can be My disciple who does not give up all his own possessions"* (Luke 14:33). Sometimes He tests us by asking us to give up the very possessions that are most important to us.

The most vivid example of this in the Bible is when the Lord instructed Abraham, *"Take now your son, your only son, whom you love, Isaac...and offer him there as a burnt offering"* (Genesis 22:2). When Abraham obeyed, demonstrating his willingness to give up his most valuable possession, God responded, *"Do not lay a hand on the boy...now I know that you fear God, because you have not withheld from me your son"* (Genesis 22:12, NIV).

When we acknowledge God's ownership, every spending decision becomes a spiritual decision. No longer do we ask, "Lord, what do You want me to do with *my* money?" It becomes, "Lord, what do You want me to do with *Your* money?" When we have this attitude and handle His money according to His wishes, spending and saving decisions become as spiritual as giving decisions.

The Lord's ownership also influences how we care for possessions. For example, because the Lord is the owner of where we live, we want to please Him by keeping His home or apartment cleaner and in better repair!

RECOGNIZING GOD'S OWNERSHIP

Our culture—the media, even the law—says that what you possess, you own. Acknowledging God's ownership requires a transformation of thinking—never an easy prospect. It's easy to give intellectual assent to the idea that "God owns all I have," but still live as if this weren't true at all.

Here are a number of practical suggestions to help us recognize God's ownership.

- For the next 30 days, meditate on 1 Chronicles 29:11-12 when you first awake and just before going to sleep.
- Be careful in the use of personal pronouns; consider substituting "the" or "the Lord's" for "my," "mine," and "ours." For instance, you might speak of *the* car instead of *my* car. Or you might refer to "the *Lord's* money" instead of "*our* money."
- For the next 30 days, ask the Lord to make you aware of His ownership—in ways large and small. Establish the habit of acknowledging the Lord's ownership every time you purchase an item.

Recognizing the Lord's ownership is important in learning contentment. When you believe you own a particular possession, circumstances surrounding it will affect your attitude. If it's favorable, you will be happy, if it's a difficult circumstance, you will be discontent.

Shortly after Jim came to grips with God's ownership, he purchased a car. He had driven the car only two days before someone rammed into the side of it. Jim's first reaction was, "Lord, I don't know why You want a dent in Your car, but now You've got a big one!" Jim was learning contentment!

CONTROL

Besides being Creator and Owner, God is ultimately in control of every event. In Scripture, we read: *"We adore you as being in control of everything"* (1 Chronicles 29:11, TLB). *"Whatever the LORD pleases, He does, in heaven and in earth"* (Psalm 135:6). In the book of Daniel, King Nebuchadnezzar stated: *"I praised the Most High; I honored and glorified Him who lives forever.... He does as He pleases with the powers of heaven and the peoples of the earth. No one can hold back His hand or say to him: 'What have you done?'"* (Daniel 4:34-35, NIV).

The Lord is also in control of difficult events. *"I am the LORD, and there is no other, the One forming light and creating darkness, causing well-being and creating calamity; I am the LORD who does all these"* (Isaiah 45:6-7).

It's important for us to realize that our heavenly Father uses even seemingly devastating circumstances for ultimate good in the lives of the godly. *"We know that God causes all things to work together for good to those who love God, to those who are called according to His purpose"* (Romans 8:28). The Lord allows difficult circumstances to enter our lives for at least three reasons: (1) to develop our character, (2) to accomplish His intentions, and (3) to lovingly discipline us when needed. We will examine this in greater detail in the Week 8—Crisis & Perspective section.

GOD IS OUR PROVIDER

The Lord promises to provide for our needs. *"Seek first His kingdom and His righteousness, and all these things* [food and clothing] *shall be given to you"* (Matthew 6:33, NIV).

The same Lord who fed manna to the children of Israel during their 40 years of wandering in the wilderness, and who satisfied the hunger of 5,000 with only five loaves and two fish has promised to meet all of our needs. This is the same Lord who told Elijah, *"I have commanded the ravens to provide for you.... The ravens brought him bread and meat in the morning and bread and meat in the evening"* (1 Kings 17:4, 6).

GOD IS BOTH PREDICTABLE AND UNPREDICTABLE.

God is totally predictable in His faithfulness to provide for our needs. What we can't predict is *how* He will provide. He uses different and often surprising means to care for us. He might meet our current need through an increase in income or an unexpected gift. On the other hand, He might choose to provide an opportunity to stretch limited resources through money-saving purchases. Then again, He might meet our needs through some circumstance that we couldn't even imagine right now. Regardless of how He chooses to provide for our needs, He is completely reliable.

Charles Allen tells a story that illustrates this. As World War II was drawing to a close, the Allied armies gathered up many orphans and placed them in camps where they were well-fed. But despite excellent care, the orphans were afraid and slept poorly.

Finally, a doctor came up with a solution. When the children were put to bed, he gave each of them a piece of bread to hold. Any hungry children could get more to eat, but when they were finished, they would still have this piece of bread just to hold—not to eat. This practice produced wonderful results. The children went to bed knowing instinctively they would have food to eat the next day, and that simple guarantee gave them restful sleep.

Similarly, the Lord has given us His guarantee—our "piece of bread." As we cling to His promises of provision, we can relax and be content. *"My God shall meet all your needs according to his glorious riches in Christ Jesus"* (Philippians 4:19, NIV).

NEEDS VERSUS WANTS

The Lord instructs us to be content when our basic needs are met. "*If we have food and clothing, we will be content*" (1 Timothy 6:8, NIV). It's important to understand the difference between a need and a want. Needs are the **basic necessities of life** —food, clothing, and shelter. Wants are **anything in excess of needs**. The Lord may allow us to have our wants, but He has not promised to provide *all* of them.

GETTING TO KNOW GOD

God, as He is revealed in the Bible, is much different than most people imagine. We tend to shrink Him down to our human abilities and limitations, forgetting that He *"stretched out the heavens and laid the foundations of the earth"* (Isaiah 51:13). By studying the Bible we can expand our vision of who He is. The following are a few samples.

HE IS LORD OF THE UNIVERSE.

Carefully review some of His names and attributes: Creator, Almighty, eternal, all-knowing, all-powerful, awesome, Lord of lords and King of kings.

The Lord's power and ability are beyond our understanding. Astronomers estimate that there are more than 100 billion galaxies in the universe, each containing billions of stars. The distance from one end of a galaxy to the other is often measured in millions of light years. Though our sun is a relatively small star, it could contain more than one million earths, and it has temperatures of 20 million degrees at its center. Isaiah wrote, *"Lift up your eyes on high and see who has created these stars.... He calls them all by name; because of the greatness of His might and the strength of His power, not one of them is missing"* (Isaiah 40:26).

HE IS LORD OF THE NATIONS.

God established the nations. Acts 17:26 says, *"He* [the Lord]*...scattered the nations across the face of the earth. He decided beforehand which should rise and fall, and when. He determined their boundaries"* (TLB).

God is far above all national leaders and powers. Isaiah 40:21-23 tells us, *"Do you not know? Have you not heard? ...It is He who sits above the circle of the earth, and its inhabitants are like grasshoppers.... He it is who reduces rulers to nothing, who makes the judges of the earth meaningless."* From Isaiah 40:15, 17 we read, *"The nations are like a drop from a bucket, and are regarded as a speck of dust on the scales.... All the nations are as nothing before Him."*

HE IS LORD OF THE INDIVIDUAL.

Psalm 139:3-4, 16 reveals God's involvement with each of us as individuals. *"You are familiar with all my ways. Before a word is on my tongue you know it completely, O Lord. ...All the days ordained for me were written in your book before one of them came to be"* (NIV). The Lord is so involved in our lives that He reassures us, *"The very hairs of your head are all numbered"* (Matthew 10:30). Our heavenly Father is the One who knows us the best and loves us the most.

God hung the stars in space, fashioned the earth's towering mountains and mighty oceans, and determined the destiny of nations. Jeremiah observed: *"Nothing is too difficult for You"* (Jeremiah 32:17).

Let's hold on to that thought for just a few seconds longer.

What in all the world, what in our lives and our current circumstances is "too difficult" for Him? N-O-T-H-I-N-G. The God who takes note of every hair follicle on every person throughout the whole world knows your situation, your needs, and even the deepest, unexpressed desires of your heart intimately. Nothing in this study is more important than catching the vision of who God is and what responsibilities He retains in our finances.

SUMMARY OF GOD'S PART

The Lord did not design people to shoulder the responsibilities that only He can carry. Jesus said, *"Come to Me, all who are weary and heavy-laden, and I will give you rest. Take My yoke upon you.... For My yoke is easy, and My burden is light"* (Matthew 11:28-30). Come to Me! God has assumed the burdens of ownership, control, and provision. For this reason, His yoke is easy and we can rest and enjoy the peace of God—if we only will.

For most of us, the primary problem is failing to consistently recognize God's part. Our culture believes that God plays no part in financial matters, and we have, in some measure, been influenced by that view.

Another reason for this difficulty is that God has chosen to be invisible. Anything that is "out of sight" tends to become "out of mind." We get out of the habit of recognizing His ownership, control, and provision.

After learning God's part, you might wonder whether He's left any responsibilities for us. The simple answer is YES. The Lord has given us great responsibility.

OUR PART

The word that best describes our part is *steward.* A steward is a manager of someone else's stuff. The Lord has given us the authority to be stewards. *"You made him ruler over the works of your* [the Lord's] *hands; you put everything under his feet"* (Psalm 8:6, NIV).

Our responsibility is summed up in this verse: *"It is required of stewards that one be found faithful"* (1 Corinthians 4:2). Before we can be faithful, however, we have to grasp what we're required to do. Just as the purchaser of a complicated piece of machinery studies the manufacturer's manual to learn how to operate it, we need to examine the Creator's handbook—the Bible—to determine how He wants us to handle His possessions.

As we begin to study our responsibilities, it's important to remember that God loves and cares for us deeply. He is a God of mercy and grace. He has given us these principles because He wants the best for us. Most people discover areas in which they have not been faithful. Don't become discouraged. Simply seek to apply faithfully what you learn.

Now, let's examine two important elements of our responsibility.

1. BE FAITHFUL WITH WHAT WE ARE GIVEN.

We are to be faithful regardless of how much God entrusts to us—whether it's a fortune or a handful of coins. The parable of the talents (a talent was a sum of money) illustrates this. *"It will be like a man going on a journey, who called his servants and entrusted his property to them. To one he gave five talents of money, to another two talents, and to another one talent*" (Matthew 25:14-15, NIV).

When the owner returned, he held each one responsible for faithfully managing his money. The owner praised the faithful servant who received five talents: *"Well done, good and faithful servant. You were faithful with a few things, I will put you in charge of many things; enter into the joy of your master"* (Matthew 25:21).

Interestingly, the servant who had been given two talents received the identical reward as the one who had been given five (see Matthew 25:23). The Lord rewards faithfulness, regardless of the amount over which we are responsible.

We are required to be faithful whether we are given much or little. As someone once said, "It's not what I would do if a million dollars were my lot; it's what I am doing with the ten dollars I've got."

2. BE FAITHFUL IN EVERY AREA.

God wants us to be faithful in handling *all* of our money. Unfortunately, most Christians have been taught how to handle only ten percent of their income God's way—the area of giving. And although this is crucial, so is the other 90 percent, which they frequently handle from the world's perspective.

Study this diagram.

As a result of not being taught to handle money biblically, many Christians have developed wrong attitudes toward possessions. This often causes them to make poor financial decisions—with painful consequences. Hosea 4:6 reads, *"My people are destroyed for lack of knowledge."*

BENEFITS OF HANDLING MONEY FAITHFULLY

The faithful steward enjoys three benefits.

1. MORE INTIMATE FELLOWSHIP WITH JESUS CHRIST

Remember what the master said to the servant who had been faithful with his finances: *"Enter into the joy of your master"* (Matthew 25:21). We can enter into closer fellowship with our Lord when we are faithful with the possessions He has given us.

Someone once told me that the Lord often allows a person to teach a subject because the teacher desperately needs it! That has certainly been true for me. I have never met anyone who had more wrong-headed attitudes about money or who handled money more contrary to the Bible than I did. And yet when I began to apply the truths set forth in these pages, I experienced a dramatic improvement in my fellowship with the Lord—exactly as He intended.

2. THE DEVELOPMENT OF CHARACTER

God uses money to refine character. As David McConaughy explained almost 100 years ago in his book, Money the Acid Test (written in 1918), "Money, most common of temporal things, involves uncommon and eternal consequences. Even though it may be done quite unconsciously, money molds people in the process of getting it, saving it, spending it, and giving it. Depending on how it's used, it proves to be a blessing or a curse. Either the person becomes master of the money, or the money becomes the master. Our Lord uses money to test our lives and as an instrument to mold us into the likeness of Himself."

All through the Bible there is a correlation between the development of people's character and how they handle money. Money is regarded as an index of a person's true character. You've no doubt heard the expression, "Money talks," and indeed it does. You can tell a lot about a person's character by examining his or her bank and credit card statements. Why? *Because we spend our money on the things that are most important to us.*

3. HAVING OUR FINANCES IN ORDER

As we apply God's principles to our finances, we will begin to get out of debt, spend more wisely, start saving for our future, and give even more to the work of Christ.

PRINCIPLES OF FAITHFULNESS

1. IF WE WASTE POSSESSIONS, THE LORD MAY REMOVE US AS STEWARDS.

"There was a certain rich man who had a manager [steward], *who was reported to him as squandering his possessions. And he called him and said to him, 'What is this I hear about you? Give an account of your management, for you can no longer be* [steward]'" (Luke 16:1-2).

Two principles emerge from this passage. First, when we waste our possessions, it eventually becomes public knowledge, and creates a poor testimony. Sooner or later, the word will get out. "[The steward] *was reported to him as squandering his possessions."* Second, the Lord may remove us as stewards if we squander what He has given us.

A businessman earned a fortune in just three years, and then went on a spending spree. Two years later he informed his staff that he had little left, and everyone would need to economize. Shortly thereafter, he left for an expensive vacation and had his personal office lavishly renovated. The Lord soon removed this man from the privilege of being steward over much, and today he is on the verge of bankruptcy.

If you waste the possessions entrusted to you, you may not be given more.

2. WE MUST BE FAITHFUL IN LITTLE THINGS.

"He who is faithful in a very little thing is faithful also in much; and he who is unrighteous in a very little thing is unrighteous also in much" (Luke 16:10).

How will you know if your son will take good care of his first car? Observe how he cared for his bicycle. How do you know if a salesperson will do a competent job of serving a large client? Evaluate how she serves a small client. If we have the character to be faithful with small things, the Lord knows He can trust us with greater responsibilities. Small things are small things, but faithfulness with a small thing is a big thing.

3. WE MUST BE FAITHFUL WITH OTHERS' POSSESSIONS.

Faithfulness with another's possessions in some measure will determine how much you are given. *"If you have not been faithful in the use of that which is another's, who will give you that which is your own?"* (Luke 16:12).

This is a principle that's often overlooked. One of the most faithful men I know rented a vehicle from a friend and damaged it in an accident. He told the owner what happened, and then delivered the vehicle to the owner's mechanic with these instructions: "Make it better than it was before the accident, and I'll be responsible for the bill." What an example!

When someone allows you to use something, are you careful to return it promptly and in good shape? Are you careless with your employer's office supplies? Do you waste electricity when you're staying in a hotel room? Some people have not been entrusted with more because they have been unfaithful with the possessions of others.

God promises to do His part in our finances; our part is to grow in faithfulness.

LIST YOUR ASSETS

Complete **List Your Assets** to get a picture of what your overall possessions look like. It is not necessary to be precise to the penny; rather, estimate the value of each asset as if you had to sell it soon.

Date: January 20, 2011

Assets (current value)	
Cash on hand/Checking Account	$1,250
Savings	$1,500
Stocks and bonds	$1,250
Cash value of life insurance	$ 0
Coins	$ 240
Home	$155,000
Other real estate	$ 0
Mortgages/Notes receivable	$ 0
Business valuation	$ 0
Automobiles	$11,000
Other Vehicles	$ 0
Furniture	$3,000
Computers & Gear	$1,000
Jewelry	$ 400
Other personal property	$ 600
Pension/Retirement Accounts	$21,000
Other Assets	$ 0
Total Assets:	$196,250

SAMPLE

LIST YOUR ASSETS

Date____________________

Assets (current value)

Cash on hand/Checking account	$________________
Savings	$________________
Stocks and bonds	$________________
Cash value of life insurance	$________________
Coins	$________________
Home	$________________
Other Real Estate	$________________
Mortgages/Notes receivable	$________________
Business valuation	$________________
Automobilcs	$________________
Other Vehicles	$________________
Furniture	$________________
Computer & electronic equipment	$________________
Jewelry	$________________
Other Personal Property	$________________
Pension/Retirement	$________________
Other Assets	$________________
Total Assets	$________________

THE DEED

To help recognize God's ownership of possessions, we will transfer the ownership of our possessions to Him. We will use a Deed, because one is often used to transfer property. This deed is not legally binding; it is solely for your use. By completing the Deed, you will establish a time when you acknowledge God's ownership.

Here are the directions to complete it.

1. Insert today's date at the top of the Deed. Then print your name in the space after "From," because you are transferring ownership of your possessions.
2. There is a large blank space following the sentence, "I (we) transfer to the Lord the ownership of the following possessions." Please pray about the possessions you wish to acknowledge that God owns, and write them in the space.
3. In the lower right-hand corner, there are two blank lines under the heading "Stewards." This is the space for your signature. If you are married, both you and your spouse should sign. In the lower left-hand corner there are two blank lines for the signatures of witnesses. Have others in your group witness your signature to help hold you accountable to recognize God as owner.

THIS DEED, MADE THE 5TH DAY OF NOVEMBER, 2013,

FROM: MATT AND MICHELLE

TO: THE LORD

I (WE) TRANSFER TO THE LORD THE OWNERSHIP OF THE FOLLOWING POSSESSIONS:

HOME	ENTERTAINMENT CENTER
AUTOMOBILE	OUR BUSINESS
CLOTHES	WEDDING RINGS
SAVINGS ACCOUNT	CHILDREN'S EDUCATION FUND
FURNITURE	PIANO
RENTAL PROPERTY	INVESTMENTS
RETIREMENT ACCOUNT	STOCK OPTIONS
COMPUTER AND GEAR	INVESTMENTS

WITNESSES WHO WILL HELP HOLD US ACCOUNTABLE TO RECOGNIZE THE LORD'S OWNERSHIP:

IMA WATCHIN

NOSIT-ALL

SIGNED BY THE STEWARDS OF THE POSSESSIONS ABOVE:

Matt

Michelle

THIS IS NOT A BINDING LEGAL DOCUMENT AND CANNOT BE USED TO TRANSFER PROPERTY.

This Deed, made the

______ day of ____________, 20__,

From:

To: The Lord

I (We) transfer to the Lord the ownership of the following possessions:

Witnesses who will help hold us accountable to recognize the Lord's ownership:

____

____

Signed by the stewards of the possessions above:

____

____

This is not a binding legal document and cannot be used to transfer property.

BUDGETING (SPENDING PLAN) OPTIONS

I prefer to call a budget a "Spending Plan" because many people are uneasy when considering a budget. It's often viewed as something that will mean a loss of freedom and endless hours of monotonous bookkeeping. But if properly understood and used, it can be enormously helpful. Because people have different preferences, we offer you three Spending Plan options.

COMPASS—PENCIL & PAPER

If you prefer a traditional handwritten Spending Plan, we've got one that really works. And don't forget to use a pencil instead of a pen when filling it out so that you can make changes easily.

COMPASS—ELECTRONIC SPREADSHEETS

Download these files by logging on to **www.compass1.org**, click on Small Group Studies Tools & Resources and then click on the Navigating Study *Student and Facilitator Tools*.

MONEY LOUNGE—ONLINE BUDGETING

Money Lounge™ has developed a *free* and effective online tool that provides a quick and easy way to create your Spending Plan. Simply answer a series of questions to begin, and then Money Lounge™ will help you get it to balance and stay balanced over the long run.

Money Lounge™ uses Mint™ (**www.mint.com**), the world's most popular free online Spending Plans. Mint tracks your spending, provides smart phone apps, sends you text or email alerts, and offers many reporting features to help you stay on top of your spending.

Log in at **www.compass1.org**, click on Small Group Studies Tools & Resources, then click on the Navigating Study Student and Facilitator Tools.

STARTING YOUR SPENDING PLAN

Each week, you'll be working on creating and using your Spending Plan. If you choose to use either the Compass "Pencil and Paper" or the Compass "Electronic Spreadsheets," we'll walk you through a step-by-step explanation of how to do it in this workbook.

If you are using the Money Lounge™ online budget, you'll learn how to start and keep using it at **compass1.org** when you click on Small Group Studies Tools & Resources and then click on the Navigating Study Student and Facilitator Tools.

COMPASS SPENDING PLAN RECORD INCOME & SPENDING

If you're using a Compass Spending Plan, it's important to record your income and spending the next 30 days to understand what you are actually earning and spending.

We recommend that you carry something with you to record your transactions. As an alternative, save your receipts and enter them into the 30 Day Tracking form daily. It's designed with one column for income and 12 columns for spending categories. It's also available electronically by logging on to **www.compass1.org** clicking on Small Group Studies Tools & Resources and then click on the Navigating Study Student and Facilitator Tools.

Income: Every time you receive income, record the amount on the 30 Day Tracking form in the Income column under the date you receive it.

Spending: Each time you spend, record the amount under the appropriate spending category.

Spending Categories: The detailed list of spending categories on pages 46-47 is designed to assist you as you decide where to categorize your purchases.

Study the sample 30 Day Tracking form and ask your small group Facilitators any questions you may have. Remember, if you are using the Money Lounge™ online budget, please disregard the Record Income & Spending explanation. Log on to **www.compass1.org**, click on Small Group Studies Tools & Resources and then click on the Navigating Study Student and Facilitator Tools.

30 Day Tracking

Month: September Year: 2011

CATEGORY	INCOME	GIVING	TAXES	SAVE/INVEST	HOUSING	FOOD
DATE						
1	2,100	100	350	100	860	
2						
3						30
4						
5						
6						
7						90
8		100			43	
9						
10	25					
11						
12						
13						
14						10
15						
15 Day Subtotal	2,125	200	350	100	903	130
16	2,100	100	350	100		
17						
18						41
19						
20					7	
21						
22						
23		100				
24						
25						
26					60	
27						85
28	25					
29	25					
30		100				10
(31)						
30 Day Total	4,275	500	700	200	970	266

SAMPLE

TRANSPORTATION	CLOTHING	MED./HEALTH	EDUCATION	PERSONAL	ENT./VAC.	DEBT
23					14	
				78		
12		35				
				35		
			190		15	
	40					120
				12		
25						
				9		
			12		11	25
60	40	35	202	134	40	145
		25				
				34		
	15					
					16	
24				17		20
26				6		
	25			23	20	
		5				80
10			12	87	8	50
120	80	65	214	301	84	295

SAMPLE

30 Day Tracking

Month: ___________ Year: ________

CATEGORY	INCOME	GIVING	TAXES	SAVE/INVEST	HOUSING	FOOD
DATE						
1						
2						
3						
4						
5						
6						
7						
8						
9						
10						
11						
12						
13						
14						
15						
15 Day Subtotal						
16						
17						
18						
19						
20						
21						
22						
23						
24						
25						
26						
27						
28						
29						
30						
(31)						
30 Day Total						

TRANSPORTATION	CLOTHING	MED./HEALTH	EDUCATION	PERSONAL	ENT./VAC.	DEBT

SPENDING PLAN CATEGORIES

Income
Monthly Salary
Interest Income
Dividends
Commissions Bonuses/Tips
Retirement Income
Net Business Income
Cash Gifts
Child Support/Alimony

1. Giving
Local Church
Poor & Needy
Ministries

2. Taxes
Federal
Medicare/Social Security
State & Local Taxes

3. Saving & Investing
Emergency Savings
Auto Replacement
401k/403b/Retire Plans
College Funds
Stocks/Bonds/Other
IRA

4. Housing
Mortgage
Pre-pay Mortgage
Property Tax
Homeowners/Flood Insurance
Rent
Renters Insurance
Electricity
Lawn Care/Gardening
Water/Sanitation
Telephone/Mobile Phone
Gas
Maintenance/Pool
TV/Cable/Satellite/Internet
Pest Control/Termite Bond
HOA/Condo Dues

5. Food
Groceries
Eating Out

6. Transportation
Auto Payments
Gas & Oil
Auto Insurance
Licenses & Taxes
Repairs/Maint/Tires
Tolls/Transit Fares/Parking
OnStar/Satellite Radio
AAA/Auto Club

7. Clothing
Adults
Children/Diapers
Laundry/Dry Cleaning

8. Medical & Health
Doctor
Dentist
Prescriptions
Eye Care/Glasses
Health/Vision/Dental Insurance
Disability Insurance
Long Term Care Insurance
Deductibles
HSA/Flexible Spending

9. Education
Adult Education
Kids Tuition/Supplies
Tutoring/Lessons/Activities

10. Personal
Allowances
Child Care/Babysitting
Life Insurance
Liability Insurance
Cleaning Supplies
Toiletries/Cosmetics
Hair Care
Vitamins/Supplements
Gifts (Birthdays)
Gifts (Christmas)
Gifts (Anniversary/Weddings)
Gifts (Graduation)
Postage
Alimony/Child Support
Pet Food & Supplies
Veterinarian
Vaccinations & Prescriptions
Boarding/Pet Sitting
Tax Preparation/Legal
Sports/Hobbies
Bank Charges/Fees
Credit Card Charges/Fees
Family Pictures
Subscriptions/Dues

11. Entertainment/Vacations
Activities
Vacations/Travel/Motel
Videos/Books/Music

12. Debts
(See Debt List on pages 76-80)

3

DEBT

FACILITATORS GUIDE

"Just as the rich rule the poor, so the borrower is servant to the lender"
(Proverbs 22:7, TLB).

DEBT

Facilitators Guide for Week 3

Overview: Debt is a struggle for many and is discouraged in the Bible.

Let's Get Practical!

☐ Begin working with the **Compass—Finances God's Way Map**™ on pages 73-75.

☐ Complete the **List Your Debts & Snowball 'Em!** on pages 76-80.

☐ Continue **Recording your Income and Spending** on pages 44-45 if you are using a Compass budget. **If you're using the online Money Lounge™ budget**, log on to **www.compass1.org** click on Small Group Studies Tools & Resources and then click on the Navigating Study Student and Facilitator Tools.

Agenda

1.__________ (5 minutes) Open in prayer.

2.__________ (5 minutes) Each person individually recites from memory:

"Just as the rich rule the poor, so the borrower is servant to the lender" (Proverbs 22:7, TLB)

3.__________ (85 minutes) Begin the group discussion.

Day One (Debt)

Complete the Compass Map and List Your Debts & Snowball 'Em! on pages 76-80.

1. Do you have any questions about the map or List Your Debts & Snowball 'Em?

2. What did you learn from completing them, and how will you use this knowledge?

Read *Deuteronomy 15:4-6; Deuteronomy 28:1-2, 12* and *Deuteronomy 28:15, 43-45.*

3. According to these passages how was debt viewed in the Old Testament, and what was the reason a person got into debt (became a borrower) or got out of it (became a lender)?

[Debt was considered a curse. Being free from debt (being a lender) was a blessing. Disobedience led to debt and obedience led to getting out of debt.]

4. What is your view of debt and how do you feel about your debt situation?

Day Two (Debt)

Read *Romans 13:8* and *Proverbs 22:7.*

1. Is debt encouraged in the Bible? Why?

Romans 13:8— [We are encouraged to stay out of debt.]

Proverbs 22:7— [The debtor is servant to the lender.]

2. How do these verses apply to you personally and to your business, if you have one?

3. If you are in debt, are you committed to get out of it? If you have a plan to eliminate it, please describe the plan.

Day Three (Debt Repayment)

Read *Psalm 37:21* and *Proverbs 3:27-28.*

1. What do these verses say about debt repayment, and why do you think God gave us these principles?

Psalm 37:21— [A person who borrows but does not repay debts is called "wicked."]

Proverbs 3:27-28— [Pay debts promptly if you have the resources. Many delay repayment as long as possible, but this is not biblical.]

2. Is this how you repay your debt? If not, what steps will you take to begin?

* *Facilitator,* you should have approximately **one hour** of class time remaining.

Day Four (Getting out of debt)

Read *2 Kings 4:1-7.*

1. What principles on getting out of debt can you identify from this passage?

[Seek the counsel of godly people, as well as the Lord's help and direction. His supernatural intervention is required whether He answers quickly, as in the case of the widow, or more slowly over time. We should use whatever resources are available—however small—in an effort to get out of debt. Involve the entire family in your effort to get out of debt.]

2. How can you apply them to your current situation?

Day Five (Cosigning)

Read *Proverbs 22:26-27* and *Proverbs 17:18.*

1. What does the Bible say about cosigning (striking hands, surety) and how does this apply to you?

Proverbs 22:26-27— [Do not cosign. It may cause you to lose assets you need.]

Proverbs 17:18— [It is poor judgment to cosign.]

Read *Proverbs 6:1-5.*

2. If someone has cosigned, what should he or she attempt to do?

[If we have cosigned, we are to humbly and diligently seek the release of our obligation.]

Day Six (the Notes)

Read the Debt Notes on pages 56-72.

1. What did you learn about debt that proved to be especially helpful?

2. How will you implement what you learned?

3. I will take the following *action* as a result of this week's study:

Remaining Agenda

1. __________ (10 minutes) Play the Week 3 segment of the *Navigating Your Finances* DVD.

2. __________ (10 minutes) Note in the Prayer Logs requests and answers to prayer.

3. __________ (5 minutes) End in prayer.

Reminder for Facilitators:

- In order to more consistently recognize God's ownership, encourage your students to continue meditating on *1 Chronicles 29:11-12.*
- Contact each participant this week and note this in the Care Log.
- Remind the students to visit Compass' web site at **www.compass1.org** and click on "Resources" for more practical assistance in getting out of debt.

DEBT NOTES

Please read *after* completing Day 5 homework.

The amount of debt in our nation has *exploded*—government debt, business debt, and personal debt. We are drowning in an ocean of red ink. More than 1 million individuals a year file bankruptcy. And even more sobering, a Gallup Poll found that a majority of divorces are caused in part by financial tension in the home.

These sorts of financial tensions often result from believing the "Gospel According to Madison Avenue." You've heard it ten thousand times: Buy now and pay later with easy monthly payments. We all know that nothing about those monthly payments is easy. Advertisers fail to tell us the whole truth, leaving out one little word—*Debt.*

WHAT IS DEBT?

The dictionary defines debt as "money that a person is obligated to pay to another." Debt includes bank loans, money borrowed from relatives, the home mortgage, past-due medical bills, and money owed to credit card companies. Bills that come due, such as the monthly electric bill, aren't considered debt if they're paid on time.

WHAT DEBT REALLY COSTS

We need to understand the real cost of debt. Assume you have $5,560 in credit card debt at an 18 percent interest rate. This would cost you $1,000 in interest annually. Check out the chart below.

1. Amount of interest you paid

Year 10	Year 20	Year 30	Year 40
$10,000	$20,000	$30,000	$40,000

2. What you would accumulate on $1,000 invested annually earning 10 percent

Year 10	Year 20	Year 30	Year 40
$17,072	$63,286	$188,386	$527,039

3. How much the lender earns from your interest payment at 18 percent

Year 10	Year 20	Year 30	Year 40
$23,521	$146,628	$790,948	$4,163,213

You can see what lenders have known for a long time: the eye-popping impact of compounding interest working *for* them. If they earn 18 percent, they will accumulate more than $4 million on your $1,000 a year for 40 years! Is it any wonder credit card companies are eager for you to become one of their borrowers?

Now compare the $40,000 you paid in interest over 40 years with the $527,039 you would have accumulated if you had earned 10 percent on $1,000 each year. The monthly income on $527,039 earning 10 percent—without ever touching the principal—is $4,392!

Debt has a much higher cost than many realize. Stop to consider this: When you assume debt of $5,560 and pay $1,000 a year in interest versus earning a 10 percent return on that $1000, it actually costs you $527,039 over 40 years. The next time you find yourself tempted to purchase something with debt, ask yourself if the long-term benefits of staying out of debt outweigh the short-term benefits of the purchase.

THE OTHER COSTS OF DEBT

Debt often increases stress, which contributes to mental, physical, and emotional fatigue. It can stifle creativity and harm relationships. Many people raise their lifestyle through debt, only to discover that its burden then controls their lifestyle.

WHAT THE BIBLE SAYS ABOUT DEBT

While Scripture doesn't specifically call debt a sin, it strongly discourages it.

Remember, God loves us and has given us these principles for our benefit. Read the first portion of Romans 13:8 from several different translations: *"Owe no man anything"* (KJV). *"Let no debt remain outstanding"* (NIV). *"Pay all your debts"* (TLB). *"Owe nothing to anyone"* (NASB). *"Keep out of debt and owe no man anything"* (AMPLIFIED). Any questions about God's view of debt?

Here's why the Lord wants you debt-free.

1. DEBT IS CONSIDERED SLAVERY.

Proverbs 22:7 reads: *"Just as the rich rule the poor, so the borrower is servant to the lender"* (TLB). When we're in debt, we're a servant to the lender. And the deeper we are in debt, the more like servants we become. We don't have the freedom to decide where to spend our income, because it's already obligated to meet our debt payments.

In 1 Corinthians 7:23, Paul writes, *"You were bought with a price; do not become slaves of men."* Our Father made the ultimate sacrifice by giving His Son, the Lord Jesus Christ, to die for us. And He now wants His children free to serve Him rather than lenders.

2. DEBT WAS CONSIDERED A CURSE.

In the Old Testament, being out of debt was one of the promised rewards for obedience.

"If you diligently obey the LORD your God, being careful to do all His commandments which I command you today, the LORD your God will set you high above all the nations of the earth. All these blessings will come upon you…. You shall lend to many nations, ***but you shall not borrow****"* (Deuteronomy 28:1-2, 12, emphasis added).

On the other hand, debt was listed among the curses for disobedience. *"If you do not obey the LORD your God, to observe to do all His commandments and His statutes with which I charge you today, that all these curses will come upon you and overtake you…. The alien who is among you shall rise above you higher and higher, but you will go down lower and lower. He shall lend to you, but you will not lend to him; he shall be the head, and you will be the tail"* (Deuteronomy 28:15, 43-44).

In God's view, then, being in debt moves you from a head position in life to the tail end!

3. DEBT PRESUMES UPON TOMORROW.

When we get into debt, we're assuming that we will earn enough in the future to repay it. But can we really assume such a thing? We plan for our jobs to continue or our investments to be profitable. The Bible strongly cautions us against such presumption: *"You who say, 'Today or tomorrow, we shall go to such and such a city, and spend a year there and engage in business and make a profit.' Yet you do not know what your life will be like tomorrow.... Instead, you ought to say, 'If the Lord wills, we shall live and also do this or that'"* (James 4:13-15).

4. DEBT MAY DENY GOD AN OPPORTUNITY.

Financial author Ron Blue tells of a young man who wanted to go to seminary to become a missionary. The young man had no money and thought the only way he could afford seminary was to secure a student loan. However, this would have left him with about $40,000 of debt by the time he graduated. He knew a missionary's salary would never be able to repay that much debt.

After a great deal of prayer, he decided to enroll without the aid of a loan, trusting the Lord to meet his needs. Several years later, he graduated without borrowing anything. Just as important, he had grown in his faith and in his appreciation for how God could provide his needs. This was the most valuable lesson learned in seminary as he prepared for life on the mission field.

BORROWING

The Bible is silent on when we can owe money. In our opinion, it is permissible to owe money for a home mortgage or for your business or vocation. This "permissible debt," however, should meet three criteria.

- The item purchased should be an asset, with the potential to appreciate or produce an income.
- The value of an item must exceed the amount owed against it.
- The debt should not be so high that repayment puts undue strain on the budget.

As we've seen during the financial and real estate crisis, there are no guarantees that home values will always appreciate or that businesses will always be profitable. So, here's the rule of thumb if you take on permissible debt: *borrow as little as possible and pay it off as quickly as possible!*

HOW TO GET OUT OF DEBT

There are three basic steps for you to become debt-free: (1) pray, (2) increase your monthly surplus, and (3) follow the Compass map. Remember, the goal is D-Day—Debtless Day—when you become totally free of debt!

1. HOW TO GET OUT OF DEBT – PRAY!

In 2 Kings 4:1-7, we read about a widow threatened with losing her sons to an aggressive creditor. When she asked the prophet Elisha for help, he told her to borrow many empty jars from her neighbors. Then the Lord multiplied her only possession—a small amount of oil—until all the jars were filled to the brim. She sold the oil and paid her debts to free her children.

The same God who provided supernaturally for the widow is interested in freeing you from debt. And He is every bit as able of meeting your needs as He was the needs of that poor widow. *The first step is to pray.* Seek the Lord's help and guidance in your journey toward Debtless Day. He may act immediately or slowly over time. In either case, prayer is essential. A trend is emerging. As people begin to eliminate debt, even little by little, the Lord blesses their faithfulness. Even if you can afford only a small monthly repayment of your debt, *do it*. The Lord is fully able to multiply your efforts.

2. HOW TO GET OUT OF DEBT – INCREASE MONTHLY SURPLUS

The larger your monthly surplus, the more money you can have available to pay down your debt. How do you increase that surplus? By increasing your income, reducing spending, and selling items you no longer need.

Earn additional income.

Many people hold jobs that simply don't pay enough to allow them to pay off their debts quickly enough. A temporary part-time job—or some creative way to earn more money—can make a huge difference in how fast you can reach D-Day.

Spend less by becoming content with what you have.

Advertisers use powerful methods to get us to buy. Frequently the message is intended to foster discontentment with what we have. An example is the American company that opened a new plant in Central America because the labor was relatively inexpensive. Everything went well until the villagers received their first paycheck; afterward they didn't return to work. Several days later, the manager went down to the village chief to determine the cause of this problem. The chief responded, "Why should we work? We already have everything we need." The plant stood idle until someone came up with the idea of sending a mail-order catalog to every villager. There hasn't been an employment problem since!

Note these three realities of our consumer-driven economy.

- The more television you watch or surfing the Web you do, the more you spend.
- The more you look at catalogs and magazines, the more you spend.
- The more you shop, the more you spend.

There is an interesting passage in 1 Timothy 6:5-6: "*...Godliness actually is a means of great gain when accompanied by contentment.*" When we are content with what we have and wait to buy until we can do it using cash—that is great gain.

Consider a radical change in lifestyle.

A growing number of people have lowered their standard of living significantly to get out of debt more quickly. Some have downsized their homes, rented apartments, or moved in with family members. Many have sold cars with large monthly payments and purchased inexpensive ones for cash. In short, they have temporarily sacrificed their standard of living so they could pay off debt more quickly. Radio host Dave Ramsey says it this way: "If you live like no one else, later you can ***live*** like no one else."

Sell what you're not using.

Evaluate your possessions to determine whether you should sell any of them to help you get out of debt more quickly. What about the clothes you no longer wear? Those fishing rods gathering dust? Is there anything you can sell to help you get out of debt?

3. HOW TO GET OUT OF DEBT – FOLLOW THE Compass—finances God's way Map™

The Compass map on pages 73-75 will help you determine which debts you ought to pay off first. At Destination 2, you focus on paying off your credit cards, because they usually have the highest interest rate. At Destination 3, you will wipe out your consumer debt: car loans, student loans, home equity loans, medical debts, and so forth. And at Destination 5, you begin to accelerate the payment of your home mortgage.

When the credit card statements arrived, it signaled the beginning of a verbal war between Alex and Nancy Popovich. They carried seven cards between them, and were using cash advances from some to satisfy the minimum monthly payments on others.

The Popoviches aren't alone. The average household with an unpaid balance has more than $9,300 in credit card debt. There has been an explosion in the number of credit cards for only one reason: *The credit card companies make a ton of money charging high interest!* The more you owe, the more interest they receive—and the more likely they can whack you with late fees and over-the-limit penalties.

Following are a few simple suggestions for paying off the plastic.

Snowball the plastic

Snowball your way out of debt. And here's how. In addition to making the minimum payments on *all* your credit cards, focus on paying off the smallest-balance-card first. You'll be encouraged to see its balance go down, down, and finally disappear!

After the first credit card is paid off, apply its payment toward the next-smallest one. After the second card is paid off, apply what you were paying on the first and second toward the third-smallest. That's the snowball in action!

When you're on a roll like this, it starts getting exciting. Those "impossible" balances that have worried you and robbed you of your peace will begin diminishing before your very eyes. So…where do you start? Prioritize your debts on the Debt List on pages 76-80. And every time you pay one of those cards off, use it as an occasion to celebrate and thank the Lord!

Perform plastic surgery

When people use credit cards rather than cash, they spend about one-third more. Why? Because it just doesn't feel like "real money"; it's just plastic. As one shopper said to another, "I like credit cards more than money because they go so much further!" If you don't pay the entire credit card balance at the end of each month, you may need to perform some plastic surgery—any good pair of scissors will do!

We started with nine credit cards. Today we carry two that we pay in full each month. To limit the temptations of additional cards, we opted out of receiving credit card offers by mail and telemarketing calls.

- To stop junk mail, call toll free 1-(888)-5OPT-OUT.
- Log on the Web site of the National Do Not Call Registry at www. donotcall.gov/ to stop telemarketers. Evening time will be much more peaceful without answering those irritating calls. **Everyone should do this!**

Lower the interest rate

There is a lot of competition among credit card companies for your business—and especially if you have a solid credit score. If your company is charging a high interest rate, phone and ask them to drop it. You may have to call several times, but 75 percent of the time, they'll lower the rate.

Another alternative is to transfer the balance to a card that charges *less* interest. Before switching to a lower-rate card, however, confirm that the new card has no transfer fee, no annual fee, and that the interest rate on transferred balances is not higher than the advertised rate. But remember, if you miss a payment or make a payment late, your interest rate will automatically skyrocket in most cases.

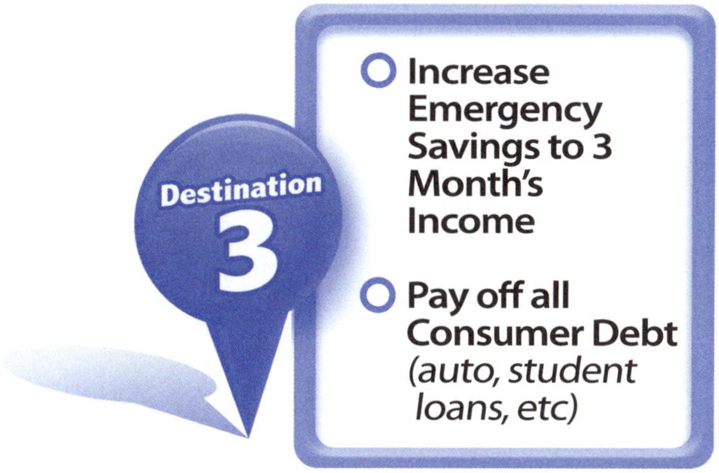

At Destination 3, you'll focus on paying off consumer loans, and one of the most common is auto debt. Seventy percent of all cars are financed, and many people never get out of car debt. It's one of the biggest obstacles for most people on their journey of financial faithfulness. Fortunately, there's a way to get out of car debt for good by following these three steps.

- Decide to keep your car at least three years longer than your car loan—and then pay off the loan.
- After your last payment, keep making the same payment, but pay it to *yourself*. Put it into an account that you will use to buy your next car.
- When you're ready to replace your car, the cash you have saved plus your car's trade-in value should be sufficient to buy a car without credit. It may not be a new car, but a low-mileage used car is a better value anyway.

Upside down

You've probably heard it said again and again: The moment you drive a car off the lot it's worth less than you paid for it. It's so true. That "new car smell" may be pleasant, but it's also incredibly expensive. Rapid depreciation is why so many new car buyers find themselves upside down on their auto loans—owing more than the car is worth. Look at the graph to see how quickly cars lose value.

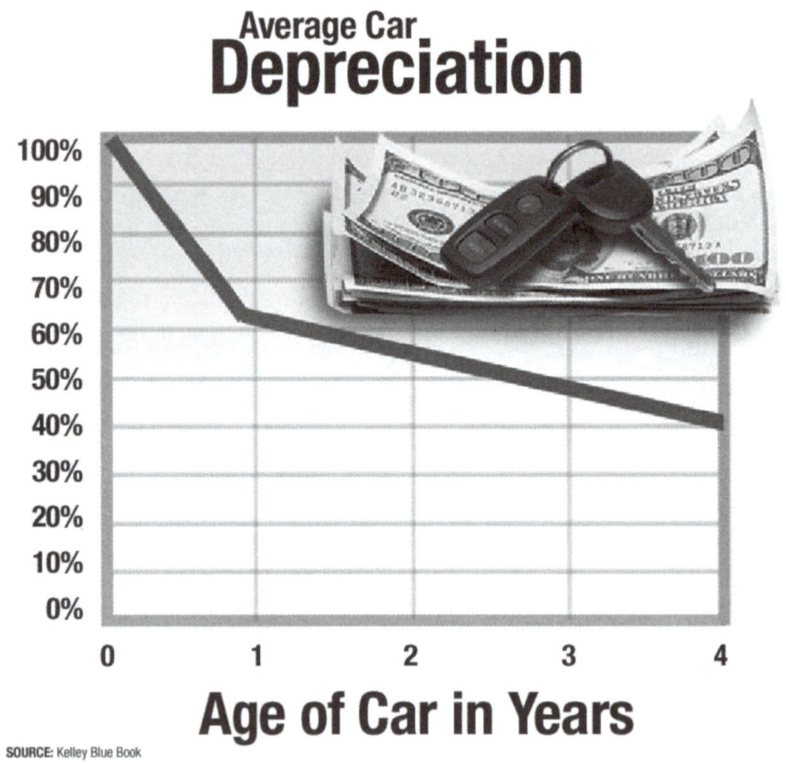

Can you believe it! The average car loses a whopping 40 percent of its value the first year—and 60 percent by year four. In other words, a new $28,000 car will lose about $17,000 of value in the first four years you own it. To get the same result, you could toss a $100 bill out the car window once a week!

For this reason, early in our marriage, Bev and I decided to buy only reliable **used** cars for cash—and drive them until the wheels fall off! Bev drove the same car for seventeen years. We used to call it

"Puff" because of the smoking exhaust pipe whenever she accelerated.

I once bought a truck that cost only a hundred dollars—and it looked it! A sympathetic neighbor borrowed it and brought it back, painted. (Suddenly it looked like a two hundred dollar truck!) While driving the truck one morning, I was enjoying a time of special worship and remembered Psalm 16:11: *"In the presence of the Lord is fullness of joy."*

You know what? In that moment, it didn't matter whether I was driving my hundred-dollar clunker or the most expensive car on the market; I could experience fullness of joy because of my relationship with Jesus Christ.

Advertisers have led us to believe that our deepest needs can be satisfied only by purchasing the newest and the best. Nothing could be further from the truth.

It's hard to overestimate the financial impact of driving debt-free cars. The average monthly new car payment is $375. If a 21-year-old drives debt-free cars and saves the $375 a month, earning an average return, he or she will accumulate about $4 million by age 65! Short-term spending sacrifices translate into enormous long-term benefits.

My advice: keep your cars as long as they are safe to drive, and buy low-mileage used cars to avoid new car depreciation.

Snowball consumer debt

After you have paid off your auto loans, focus on paying off your consumer debts in exactly the same way as you wiped out your plastic—snowball 'em. Make the minimum payments on all your consumer debts, but focus on accelerating the payment of your smallest consumer debt first. Then, after you pay off the first consumer debt, apply its payment toward the next-smallest one. After the second one is paid off, apply what you were paying on the first and second to pay off the third, and so forth.

At Destination 5, you will begin paying off your home mortgage. If you haven't yet purchased a home and want to, there are two rules of thumb for buying an affordable home:

First, put a minimum of 20 percent down payment. This will eliminate the need for expensive PMI insurance, which doesn't benefit you at all. And forget adjustable-rate mortgages; get one that's fixed rate. If you don't yet have enough saved for 20 percent down, renting usually is much cheaper than owning. So rent—and save like crazy.

Second, no more than 40 percent of your income should be spent for all housing expenses, including mortgage payments, insurance, real estate taxes, utilities, and maintenance. If housing costs exceed 40 percent, you'll find yourself continually robbing money from other spending categories to balance your budget.

PAYING OFF THE HOME MORTGAGE

When Bev and I learned God's financial truths, we became convinced that the Lord wanted us entirely out of debt, even our home. We understood this to be a *really* long-term goal because of the size of our mortgage. But we also realized that if we could pay it off, it would free up a big chunk of our income, so that we could give more generously *and* save more aggressively.

We didn't start prepaying the mortgage until we wiped out all our credit card and consumer debt. Then we focused on the home by paying an extra amount each month to reduce the principal more quickly. The longer we did it, the more excited we became. Finally, we also started applying work bonuses and income tax refunds to our mortgage.

Prepaying your mortgage can save you *tons* of interest. Log on to www.compass1.org and click on "Resources" to learn how much interest you can save by paying extra toward principal each month. If you've never looked at a chart like this before, it will knock your socks off.

Once you have decided to pay off your home, let your lender know, so they can tell you how to get proper credit for your prepayment.

Some homeowners don't want to prepay the mortgage and decrease the interest payments, reasoning that interest is one of their biggest tax deductions. But this tax advantage is overrated. If you are in the 25 percent tax bracket, for each $1,000 you pay in home interest, you save only $250 in taxes—25 percent of the $1,000 interest paid. So while there is a tax benefit, it's not as much as many think. Paying $1,000 to save $250 is not *that* great a deal.

As Bev and I discovered, paying off our home mortgage was a key step on the journey to financial faithfulness.

INVESTMENT DEBT

Should you borrow money to make an investment? In our opinion, it is permissible to borrow for an investment, but only if the investment (along with your down payment) is the sole collateral for the debt. You should not personally guarantee repayment of the debt. At first, this may appear to contradict the biblical admonition to repay our debts. But let's explore this further.

Suppose you wanted to purchase a rental property with a reasonable down payment, making sure that the house would be the sole security for the debt. You would explain to potential lenders that at your option, you would repay the loan in one of two ways: First, by giving the lender cash—making the payments. Or second, by giving the lender the property plus the down payment and any other money you had invested in the house.

Given those options, the lender must make a decision. Is the down payment sufficient? Is the rental property of adequate value?

Some investors have responded that it's impossible to locate a lender willing to loan without a personal guarantee. That, however, has not been my experience. When I was in the real estate business, I prayed for this type of financing and then knocked on lots of doors. Eventually I got it.

Because of the possibility of difficult financial events over which you have no control, be sure to limit your potential loss to the cash you invest and the asset itself. It's painful to lose your investment, but it's much more serious to jeopardize your family's needs by risking all your personal assets on investment debt.

BUSINESS DEBT

We also want to encourage you to pray about becoming debt-free in your business. Many business owners are recognizing the competitive advantage and increased stability they enjoy when they eliminate business debt.

Here is our rule of thumb on business debt: Use as *little* as possible and pay it off as *quickly* as possible.

CHURCH DEBT

The Bible doesn't specifically address whether a church may borrow money to build or expand its facility. In our opinion, such debt is permissible if the church leadership clearly senses the Lord's leading to do so. If a church borrows, we recommend that it raise as much money as possible for the down payment and establish a plan to pay off the debt as rapidly as possible. A growing number of churches have chosen to build without the use of any debt. For many of these churches, the members' faith has increased as they have observed the Lord providing the necessary funds, and they have been encouraged to become debt free themselves.

DEBT REPAYMENT RESPONSIBILITIES

Prompt payment

Many people delay paying creditors until payments are past due, even when they have the money. On this practice, however, the Bible is crystal clear. In Proverbs 3:27-28 we read: *"Do not withhold good from those to whom it is due, when it is in your power to do it. Do not say to your neighbor, 'Go, and come back, and tomorrow I will give it,' when you have it with you."*

Godly people should pay their debts and bills as promptly as they can. Some try to pay each bill the same day they receive it, to demonstrate to others that knowing Jesus Christ has made them financially responsible.

Using your savings

In our opinion, it's not smart to use *all* your savings to pay off debt. Follow the Compass map, and keep three months' living expenses set aside for emergencies.

Bankruptcy

A court can declare people bankrupt and unable to pay their debts. Depending on the type of bankruptcy, the court will either allow them to develop a plan to repay their creditors or it will distribute their property among the creditors as payment.

Should a godly person declare bankruptcy? Generally, no. Psalm 37:21 tells us, *"The wicked borrows and does not pay back."*

However, in our opinion, bankruptcy is permissible under two circumstances:

- *When a creditor or circumstances force a person into bankruptcy.* There are occasions when bankruptcy is the only viable option when the financial challenges become too extreme to reverse. That option needs to be exercised only after all others have been explored.

- *When the emotional health of the borrower is at stake.* If the debtor's emotional health is at risk because of inability to cope with the pressure of aggressive creditors, bankruptcy can be an option.

Declaring bankruptcy should never be a cavalier decision, because it remains on a credit report for *ten* years, and often impairs one's ability to obtain future credit at reasonable interest rates. Potential employers and landlords are also likely to learn of a past bankruptcy. It can haunt people for years, and although it provides relief, it's not exactly the fresh start that some advertise.

After a person goes through bankruptcy, he should seek counsel from an attorney to determine if it's legally permissible to repay the debt, even though he is not obligated to do so. If it's allowable, every effort should be made to repay the debt. For a large debt, this may be a long-term goal that is largely dependent upon the Lord supernaturally providing the resources.

COSIGNING

Cosigning relates to debt. *Anytime you cosign, you become legally responsible for the debt of another.* It's just as if you went to the bank, borrowed the money, and gave it to your friend or relative who is asking you to cosign. In effect, *you* promise to pay back the entire amount if the borrower does not.

A Federal Trade Commission study found that 50 percent of those who cosigned for bank loans ended up making the payments. And 75 percent of those who cosigned for finance company loans ended up making the payments! Those are pretty good odds that if you cosign, you'll pay. The casualty rate is so high because the professional lender knows the loan is a bad risk, and told himself, *I won't touch this loan with a ten-foot pole unless I can get someone who is financially responsible to guarantee its repayment.*

Fortunately, the Bible gives us clear direction about cosigning. Proverbs 17:18 says, *"It is poor judgment to countersign another's note, to become responsible for his debts"* (NLT). The words "poor judgment" are literally translated "destitute of mind"!

A parent often cosigns for his or her child's first automobile. We decided not to do this. We wanted to model for our children the importance of not cosigning, and to discourage them from using debt. Instead, we encouraged them to think ahead and save for the purchase of their first cars.

Already cosigned?

If you have already cosigned for a loan, the Scripture has counsel for you, too. Get out of it as fast as you can!

Proverbs 6:1-5 says, *"Son, if you endorse a note for someone you hardly know, guaranteeing his debt, you are in serious trouble. You may have trapped yourself by your agreement. Quick! Get out of it if you pos-*

sibly can! Swallow your pride; don't let embarrassment stand in the way. Go and beg to have your name erased. Don't put it off..... If you can get out of this trap you have saved yourself like a deer that escapes from a hunter, or a bird from the net" (TLB).

Please use sound judgment and never cosign.

CREDIT REPORT AND SCORE

Your credit score (FICO score) determines whether you can get credit. And your score may be high enough to get credit but not high enough to get a decent interest rate—whether you're looking for a mortgage, a car loan, or some other type of credit. Without good scores, your application to rent an apartment may be turned down. Your scores can affect your car insurance premiums and even getting a job.

Both the wife and husband have their own separate credit scores. Often, only husbands have credit in their names, with the result that wives don't have the opportunity to establish good credit on their own. This is a mistake! If a husband dies before his wife, she won't have a solid credit score—at the very time when she may need it most. Bev and I solved this problem by each securing a credit card in our name that we pay on time and in full every month. When we receive the credit card statements, we meet to review them so our communication remains intact.

A credit score is a number designed to help lenders and others measure your likelihood of making payments on time. The FICO score ranges from 300-850, with the average score around 680. Higher scores are better. FICO scores above 700 indicate a good credit risk, while scores below 600 indicate a poor risk.

A low score can lead to much higher interest rates. For example, if you apply for a 30-year home mortgage and your credit score is too low, you could pay as much as three percent more. On a $200,000 mortgage, that three percent difference will cost you $400 per month. Over the life of the loan, it adds up to $144,000!

The primary things that will harm your credit score are late payments or non-payments of bills or debts, bankruptcy, foreclosure, repossession, and bills or loans sent to collection. To improve your score, the two most important actions you can take are to pay your bills on time and reduce your total debt. Once you start doing this, your score will begin to improve in about three months. Look at the factors affecting your score.

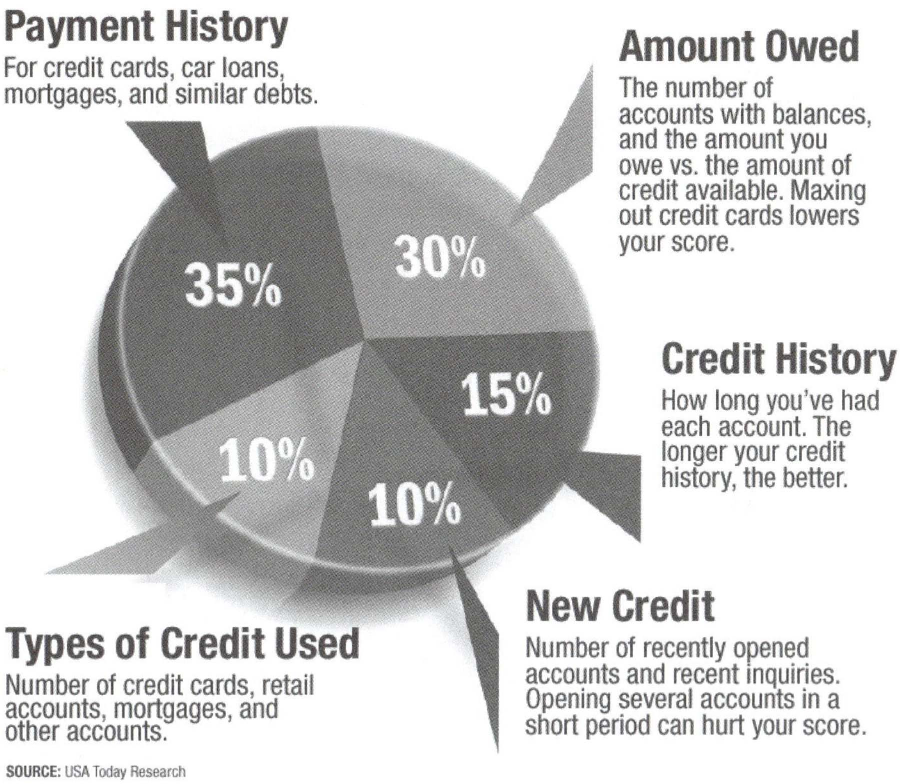

Late or missed payments, foreclosures or repossessions remain part of your credit report for seven years. You'll have to wait ten years for a bankruptcy to be removed, and fifteen years for a tax lien. Even though these remain on your credit report, over time they have less impact if you pay your bills on time and reduce your debt.

Credit report

Everyone can get a copy of their credit report and *should get a copy of their credit report* once a year from the three major credit reporting agencies: TransUnion, Equifax and Experian. You can order a free copy of your credit report by logging on to **AnnualCreditReport.com**. Carefully review it to make sure there are no mistakes or that you haven't been the victim of identity theft. The free copy of your credit report does not contain your credit score. Any of the three main credit agencies will sell you your score.

DON'T GIVE UP!

On October 29, 1941, Winston Churchill, Prime Minister of England, gave a school commencement address. World War II was devastating Europe, and England's very fate as a nation was in doubt. Churchill stood and said:

> "Never give in. Never give in. Never, never, never—in nothing, great or small, large or petty—never give in except to convictions of honor and good sense."

So I want to encourage you to *never* give up in your effort to get out of debt. It may require hard work and sacrifice, but the freedom is worth the struggle. Remember, it is on God's heart for you to become debt free.

RECOMMENDED RESOURCES

For hints on how to accumulate Emergency Saving log on to **www.compass1.org** and click on Resources

Dave Ramsey's *Financial Peace University*

Free and Clear: God's Roadmap to Debt Free Living, by Howard Dayton, Moody Publishers

Compass—*finances God's way* Map™

The Compass map is easy to understand and follow, and is a proven, step-by-step guide that works for *everyone*, regardless of your financial situation. The map answers the three big questions—financially where am I, where do I want to go, and what do I do next? The first step is to find out where you are.

Look at the map on pages 74-75. There are seven destinations on the journey. Take a few minutes and review each destination. Check off the boxes that you've already accomplished. After you have reviewed the seven destinations and checked off the boxes you have already completed, you know where you are on your journey. The next step is to determine what to do next.

The next step is simply to focus on accomplishing the *first destination you have not yet finished.*

Your Money Map

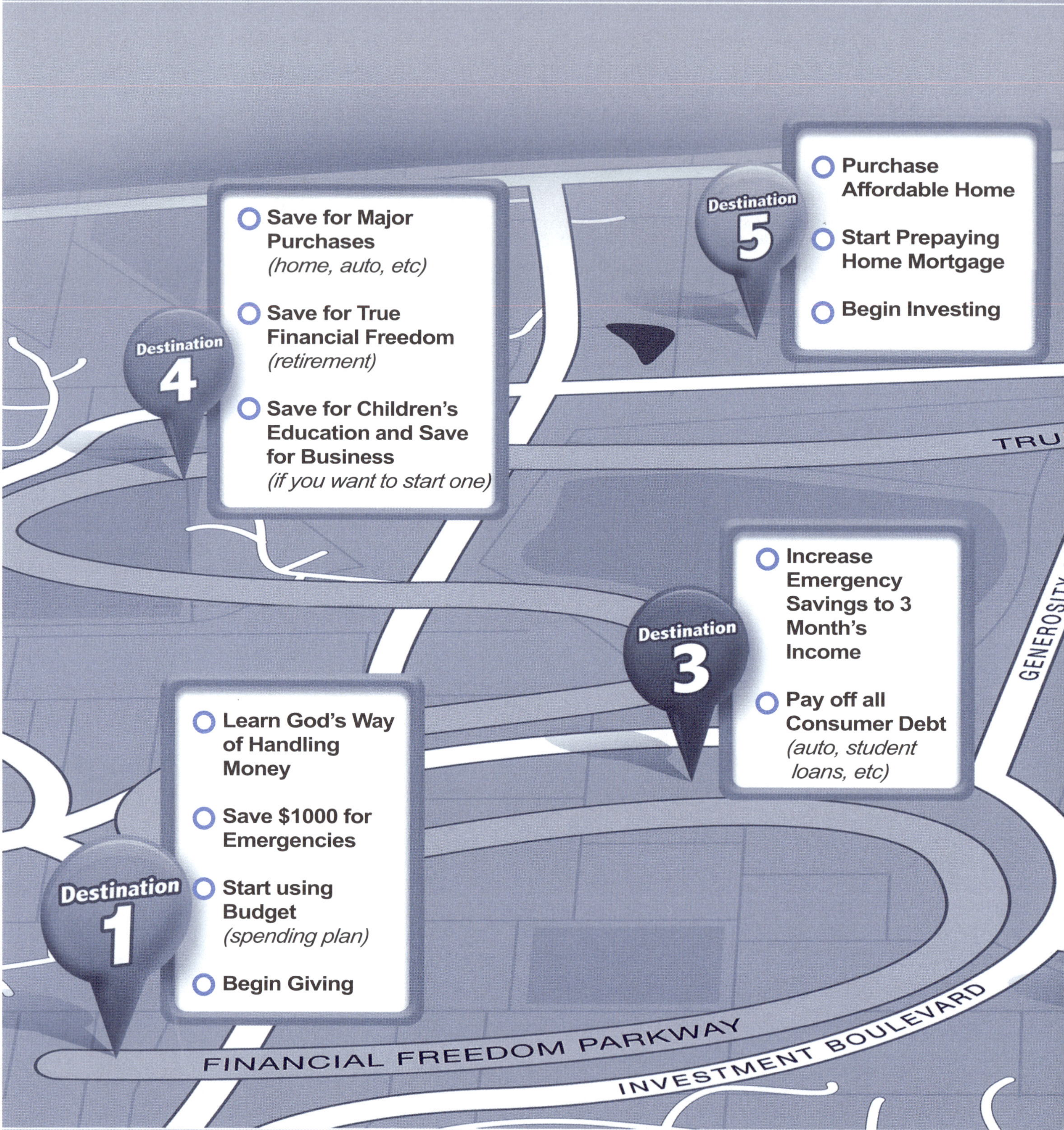

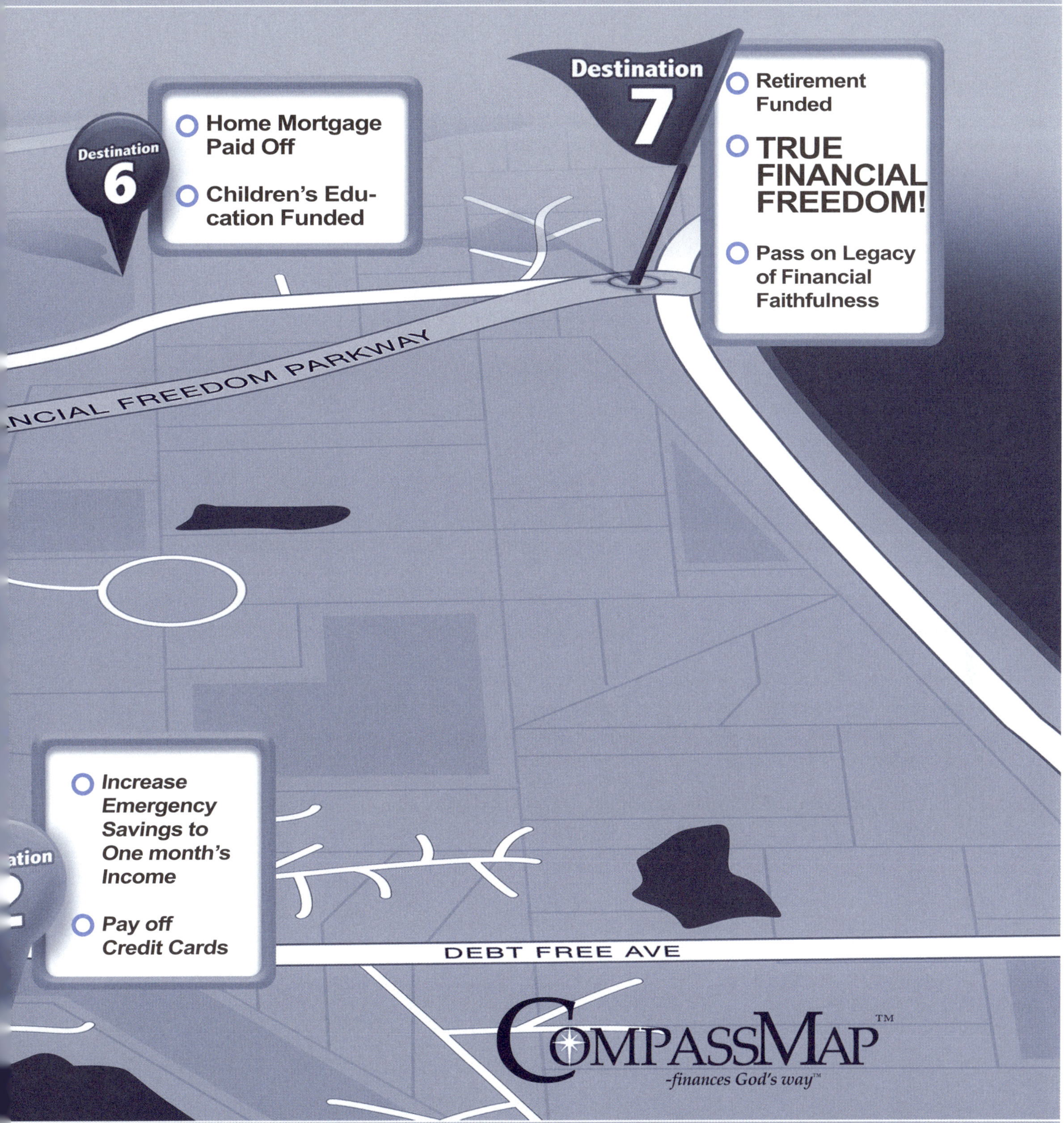
Destination
6
Home Mortgage Paid Off
Children's Edu-cation Funded
Destination
7
Retirement Funded
TRUE FINANCIAL FREEDOM!
Pass on Legacy of Financial Faithfulness
NCIAL FREEDOM PARKWAY
ation
Increase Emergency Savings to One month's Income
Pay off Credit Cards
DEBT FREE AVE
COMPASSMAP™
-finances God's way™

LIST YOUR DEBTS & SNOWBALL 'EM!

Listing your debts will assist you in compiling your debts and prioritizing repayment so you can snowball 'em! The columns are as follows:

- **Creditor** - The one to whom the debt is owed.
- **Balance Due** - The amount of the current debt.
- **Monthly Payment** - The amount of the monthly payment. If payment is due more or less often than monthly, calculate the average amount paid each month.
- **Interest Rate** - The rate of interest charged for the debt.
- **Scheduled pay-off date** - The date by which the debt will be fully paid.
- **Snowball Priority** – Number the debts in the order you are going to pay them off.

After entering each debt, add and total the monthly payment and the balance due columns.

Snowball debt

Remember how to snowball your debt as you prioritize paying them off. Make the minimum payments on all your debts, but focus on accelerating the payment of your smallest credit card debt first. Then, after you pay off the first one, apply its payment toward the next-smallest one. After the second one is paid off, apply what you were paying on the first and second to pay off the third, and so forth.

After you pay off all your plastic debt, snowball your other debts in exactly the same way.

LIST YOUR DEBTS & SNOWBALL 'EM!

Creditor	Balance Due	Monthly Payment	Interest Rate	Scheduled Pay-Off Date	Snowball Priority
Credit Card Debt					
Visa	$350	$20	12	1/2012	1
Master Card	$4,250	$80	9	8/2016	3
Sears	$2,400	$55	18	11/2014	2
Auto Loans					
Crazy Lou's Auto	$5,500	$125	10	12/2012	5
Home Mortgages					
2nd Nat'l Bank	$135,000	$850	5	7/2028	7
Medical Bills					
Bank Loans					
Last Nat'l Bank	$1,000	$50	12	1/2012	4

SAMPLE

Education Debt

Insecurity Bank	$15,000	$85	5	7/2020	6

Debt Family/Friends

Business/Investment Debt

Life Insurance Loans

SAMPLE

TOTAL DEBT $163,500 $1,265

Cosigned Loans (Contingent Debt)

Uncle Charlie	$3,500				

LIST YOUR DEBTS & SNOWBALL 'EM!

Creditor	Balance Due	Monthly Payment	Interest Rate	Scheduled Pay-Off Date	Snowball Priority
Credit Card Debt					
Auto Loans					
Home Mortgages					
Medical Bills					
Bank Loans					

Education Debt

Debt Family/Friends

Business/Investment Debt

Life Insurance Loans

TOTAL DEBT

Cosigned Loans (Contingent Debt)

4

HONESTY & COUNSEL

FACILITATORS GUIDE

"You shall not steal, nor deal falsely, nor lie to one another" (Leviticus 19:11).

HONESTY & COUNSEL

Facilitators Guide for Week 4

Overview: The Lord requires us to be totally honest. Everyone should seek counsel when they make a major financial decision. In our culture, people are discouraged from seeking counsel.

Let's Get Practical!

☐ Begin to use the **Filing System** on page 105.

☐ Complete **Determining Your Life Insurance Needs** on pages 105-107.

☐ Continue **Recording your Income and Spending** on pages 44-45 if you are using a Compass budget. **If you're using the online Money Lounge™ budget**, log on to **www.compass1.org**, click on Small Group Studies Tools & Resources and then click on the Navigating Study Student and Facilitator Tools.

Agenda

1.__________ (5 minutes) Open in prayer.

2.__________ (5 minutes) Each person individually recites from memory:

"You shall not steal, nor deal falsely, nor lie to one another" (Leviticus 19:11).

3.__________ (85 minutes) Begin the group discussion.

Day One (Honesty)

Complete Determining Your Life Insurance Needs and the Filing System on pages 105-107.

1. Do you have any questions about them?

2. What did you learn from completing Determining Your Life Insurance Needs and setting up your Filing System? How will these help on your journey to *true financial faithfulness*?

Read *Leviticus 19:11-13; Deuteronomy 25:13-16* and *Ephesians 4:25.*

3. What do these verses communicate to you about God's requirement for honesty?

Leviticus 19:11-13— [The Lord commands us to be honest.]

Deuteronomy 25:13-16— [The Lord demands honesty in our business dealings.]

Ephesians 4:25— [We are not to lie to one another.]

4. Are you consistently honest in even the smallest details? If not, what will you do to change?

Read *Proverbs 14:2.*

5. Can you practice dishonesty and still love God? Why?

[No, those who practice dishonesty hate the Lord. When people are dishonest, they are acting as if God is not able to provide exactly what they need, is incapable of discovering their dishonesty, and is powerless to discipline them. In other words, dishonest people live as if He doesn't exist.]

Read *Proverbs 26:28* and *Romans 13:9-10.*

6. According to these passages, can you practice dishonesty and still love your neighbor? Why?

[No, because dishonest people hate those they hurt. Love does no wrong to a neighbor. Because dishonesty always harms people, we cannot love and be dishonest at the same time.]

Day Two (Honesty)

Read *Psalm 15:1-5; Proverbs 20:7* and *Isaiah 33:15-16.*

1. What are some of the benefits of honesty and how have you experienced them?

Psalm 15:1-5— [More intimate fellowship with the Lord.]

Proverbs 20:7— [The children of an honest person are blessed.]

Isaiah 33:15-16— [The Lord will protect and provide for the needs of the honest.]

Read *Proverbs 3:32; Proverbs 13:11* and *Proverbs 21:6.*

2. What are some of the curses of dishonesty and how do they motivate you to a life of honesty?

Proverbs 3:32— [A dishonest person is an abomination to the Lord.]

Proverbs 13:11— [Anything obtained dishonestly will be taken away.]

Proverbs 21:6— [Obtaining wealth by lying produces only temporary gains and eventually leads to death.]

Day Three (Restitution & Bribes)

Read *Exodus 22:1-4; Numbers 5:5-8* and *Luke 19:8.*

1. What does the Bible say about restitution?

[Restitution was required under Old Testament law. Zaccheus is an example of fulfilling this obligation. Restitution involved the return of the item acquired dishonestly, plus a penalty.]

2. If you have acquired anything dishonestly, how will you make restitution?

[Ask forgiveness from the Lord, confess your dishonesty to the person harmed, and make restitution. Sometimes restitution is a delicate and complex issue. The question of how to fulfill the principle of restitution should be prayerfully answered.]

Read *Exodus 23:8* and *Proverbs 15:27.*

3. What does Scripture say about bribes?

[Never take a bribe because it will influence your judgment. The person not involved with bribes will live, but a leader who takes bribes will be overthrown.]

4. Have you ever been asked to give or take a bribe? If so, describe what happened.

* *Facilitators*, you should have about **one hour** of time remaining in class.

Day Four (Counsel)

Read *Proverbs 12:15* and *Proverbs 13:10.*

1. What are some of the benefits of seeking counsel?

Proverbs 12:15— [The person who listens to counsel is wise.]

Proverbs 13:10— [Wisdom comes to those who seek counsel, but the consequence of not seeking counsel is strife.]

2. What are some of the benefits you've experienced from seeking counsel? And what hinders you from seeking it?

Read *Psalm 16:7* and *Psalm 32:8.*

3. Does the Lord actively counsel His children? How do you seek the Lord's counsel?

[The Lord counsels us primarily through prayer, the Bible and godly people.]

Day Five (Counsel)

Read *Psalm 119:105; 2 Timothy 3:16-17* and *Hebrews 4:12.*

1. Should the Bible also serve as your counselor? Why?

[Yes, the Bible is the inspired Word of God, it is living, and provides direction for our lives.]

2. Do you consistently read and study the Bible? If not, what prevents you?

3. In your opinion, who should be the number-one human counselor of a husband? Of a wife? Why?

[The husband and wife are each other's most important human counselors.]

Read *Psalm 1:1-3* and *Proverbs 12:5*.

4. Who should you avoid as a counselor and why?

[Avoid the wicked as your counselor.]

5. Is there ever a circumstance in which you should seek the input of a person who does not know Christ? If so, when?

[In our opinion, it's permissible to seek input from those who don't know Christ when you are gathering facts. After collecting facts, solicit counsel from godly people before arriving at your decision.]

Day Six (the Notes)

Read the Honesty & Counsel Notes on pages 90-104.

1. What did you learn about honesty that will be especially helpful to you? In what way?

2. What was the most important thing you learned about counsel and how will you apply it?

3. I will take the following *action* as a result of this week's study.

Remaining Agenda

1. __________ (10 minutes) Play the Week 4 segment of the *Navigating Your Finances* DVD.
2. __________ (10 minutes) Note in the Prayer Logs requests and answers to prayer.
3. __________ (5 minutes) End in prayer.

HONESTY & COUNSEL NOTES

Please read *after* completing Day 5 homework.

This week we will examine God's perspective on *honesty* and *counsel.*

All of us have to make decisions about whether to handle money honestly. Do you tell the cashier when you receive too much change? Have you ever tried to sell something and been tempted not to tell the truth, because you might lose the sale?

HONESTY IN SOCIETY

Deciding on a course of honesty and integrity is all the more difficult because so many around us every day act dishonestly. After pumping twenty dollars' worth of gas in my truck, I asked for a receipt. When the attendant handed me a receipt for twenty-five dollars, I pointed out the mistake. His answer? "Oh, just turn it in to your company, and you'll make a fast five bucks. After all, that's what a lot of the mailmen around here do."

When I heard that, my heart sank. The verse that came immediately to mind was Judges 17:6, *"Every man did what was right in his own eyes."* People today formulate their own standards of honesty—and then change them when circumstances change.

HONESTY IN SCRIPTURE

Hundreds of verses in the Bible communicate the Lord's desire for us to be completely honest in all our dealings. For instance, Proverbs 20:23 says, *"The LORD loathes all cheating and dishonesty"* (TLB). And Proverbs 12:22 states, *"Lying lips are an abomination to the LORD."* And in Proverbs 6:16-17 we read, *"The LORD hates...a lying tongue."*

Study the following comparison between what the Scriptures teach and what our society practices concerning honesty.

ISSUE	SCRIPTURE	SOCIETY
Standard of honesty	Absolute	Relative
God's concern about honesty	He demands honesty	There is no God
The decision to be honest or dishonest is based upon	Faith in the invisible, living God	Only the facts that can be seen
Question usually asked deciding whether to be honest	Will it please God?	Will I get away with it?

The God of Truth

Truthfulness is one of God's attributes. He is repeatedly identified as the God of truth. Jesus said, *"I am…the truth"* (John 14:6). Our loving heavenly Father commands us to reflect His honest and holy character: *"Be holy yourselves also in all your behavior; because it is written, 'You shall be holy, for I am holy'"* (1 Peter 1:15-16).

In contrast to God's nature, John 8:44 describes the devil's character: *"He* [the devil] *was a murderer from the beginning, and does not stand in the truth because there is no truth in him. Whenever he speaks a lie, he speaks from his own nature, for he is a liar and the father of lies."* The Lord wants us to conform to His honest character rather than to the dishonest nature of the devil.

TOTAL HONESTY

God wants us to be completely honest for the following reasons.

We cannot practice dishonesty and love God.

Two of the Ten Commandments address honesty. *"You shall not steal.... You shall not bear false witness against your neighbor"* (Exodus 20:15-16). And Jesus told us, *"If you love Me, you will keep My commandments"* (John 14:15). We cannot disobey by practicing dishonesty and still claim to love God.

When being dishonest, we behave as if the living God doesn't even exist! It's a clear signal that we simply don't believe He is able to provide what we need, even though He has promised to do so (Matthew 6:33). We take the situation into our own hands and do it in our own dishonest way. We're also acting as if God is incapable of discovering our dishonesty and powerless to discipline us. If we really believe God will discipline us, we won't consider acting dishonestly.

At the heart of it all, honest behavior is really an issue of faith. An honest decision may look foolish in light of what we can see, but the godly person knows Jesus Christ is alive, even though invisible. Every honest decision—even the decision that may harm us in the short run—strengthens our faith and helps us grow into a closer relationship with Christ. When we choose to be dishonest, we are denying our Lord. It's impossible to love God with all our heart, soul, and mind if, at the same time, we act as if He doesn't exist. Scripture declares that the dishonest hate God. *"...He who is crooked in his ways despises Him"* (Proverbs 14:2).

Before learning God's view of honesty, I had no clue He felt so strongly about it. I was often dishonest in my financial dealings. Once I began breaking my dishonest habits, however, I realized that the Lord's primary interest in our honest behavior is so that we can experience a closer relationship with Him.

We cannot practice dishonesty and love our neighbor.

The Lord requires honesty because dishonest behavior also violates the second commandment, *"You shall love your neighbor as yourself"* (Mark 12:31). Romans 13:9-10 reads, *"If you love your neighbor as much as you love yourself you will not want to harm or cheat him...or steal from him. ...Love does no wrong to anyone"* (TLB).

When we act dishonestly, what we're really doing is stealing from another person. We may rationalize that it's a business or the government or an insurance company that is suffering the loss. Yet, if we look at the bottom line, it is the business owners or fellow taxpayers or policyholders from whom we are stealing. It's just as if we took the money from their wallets. In the final analysis, the victim is always a person.

Credibility for evangelism

Honesty enables us to demonstrate the reality of Jesus Christ to those who don't yet know Him. I will never forget the first time I told a neighbor how he could come to know Christ as his personal Savior. He angrily responded, "Well, I know a man who always goes to church and talks a lot about Jesus, but watch out if you ever get in a business deal with him! He'd cheat his own grandmother! If that's what it means to be a Christian, I don't want any part of it!"

Our actions speak louder than our words. *"Prove yourselves to be blameless and innocent, children of God above reproach in the midst of a crooked and perverse generation, among whom you appear as lights in the world"* (Philippians 2:15).

We can influence people ***for*** Jesus Christ by handling money honestly. Robert had been trying to sell a car for months when someone finally made an acceptable offer. At the last moment, however, the buyer said, "I have one condition—you don't report this sale so I won't have to pay state sales tax."

Although he was tempted, Robert responded, "I'm sorry, I can't do that because Jesus Christ is my Lord." Robert later said, "You should have seen his reaction. He almost went into shock! Then his attitude completely changed. Not only did he buy the car, but he eagerly joined my wife and me at our dinner table. Rarely have I seen anyone as open to the truth about knowing Jesus Christ."

Confirms God's direction

Proverbs 4:24-26 reads, *"Put away from you a deceitful mouth and put devious speech far from you. Let your eyes look directly ahead and let your gaze be fixed straight in front of you. Watch the path of your feet and all your ways will be established."*

What a great principle. As you are completely honest, *"all your ways will be established."* Choosing to walk the narrow path of honesty eliminates the many possible avenues of dishonesty.

"If only I'd understood that," Raymond said. "Donna and I wanted that house so much. It was our dream home. But we had too much debt to qualify for the mortgage. The only way for us to buy it was to hide some of our debts from the lender.

"It was the worst decision of our lives. Almost immediately we were unable to meet the mortgage payment, and pay our other debts, too. The pressure built and was more than Donna could stand. Our dream house ended up being a family nightmare. I not only lost the house, but nearly lost my wife."

Had Raymond and Donna been honest, their lender would not have approved the loan, and they would have been unable to purchase that particular home. Had they prayed and waited, God might have brought something more affordable, thus avoiding the pressure that almost ended their marriage. Honesty helps confirm God's direction.

Even small acts of dishonesty are harmful

God requires us to be *completely honest*, because even the smallest act of dishonesty is sin, and interrupts our fellowship with the Lord. The smallest "white lie" hardens our hearts, making our consciences increasingly insensitive to sin. This single cancer cell of small dishonesty multiplies and spreads to greater dishonesty. *"Whoever is dishonest with very little will also be dishonest with much"* (Luke 16:10, NIV).

An event in Abraham's life challenges us to be honest in small matters. The king of Sodom offered Abraham all the goods he had recovered when he had rescued the people of Sodom. But he responded, *"I have sworn to the Lord God Most High, possessor of heaven and earth, that I will not take a thread or a sandal thong or anything that is yours"* (Genesis 14:22-23).

Just as Abraham was unwilling to take so much as a thread, we challenge you to make a similar commitment. Covenant not to steal a stamp or a penny from your employer or anyone else. The people of God must be honest in even the smallest matters.

To love God, to guide our steps, and to be more effective ambassadors of His love to our family and neighbors. Is it any wonder that our Lord wants us to be completely honest?

ESCAPING THE TEMPTATION OF DISHONESTY

A friend was teaching these principles in a secular school when a young man raised his hand and said, "I think we'd all like to be honest, but I know in my heart that if the right opportunity comes along, I'm going to be dishonest."

Was that student just being cynical? No, apart from being yielded to the Holy Spirit, all of us will be dishonest. The Bible says, *"Live by the Spirit, and you will not gratify the desires of the sinful nature. For the sinful nature desires what is contrary to the Spirit, and the Spirit what is contrary to the sinful nature"* (Galatians 5:16-17, NIV).

It's human nature to act dishonestly. *"Out of men's hearts, come evil thoughts… theft…deceit"* (Mark 7:21-22, NIV). The Holy Spirit, who indwells our lives, desires us to be honest. And we need His help! Just bear in mind that the totally honest life is supernatural. To experience that life, we need to submit ourselves entirely to Jesus Christ as Lord, and allow Him to live His life through us. There is no other way.

I heartily recommend a short book by Andrew Murray titled *Humility*. It's an excellent study on yielding fully to Christ.

The following principles will help you develop the habit of honesty.

1. PRACTICE THE GOLDEN RULE.

"Do not merely look out for your own personal interests, but also for the interests of others" (Philippians 2:4). This verse is better translated, "look intently" after the interests of others.

The Lord used this passage to point out Warren's lack of concern for others just when he was about to purchase some land, taking advantage of a seller who knew nothing of its true value. Warren secretly congratulated himself, because he knew the purchase price he had offered was very low. Not once had he considered what would be fair to the seller.

Later, however, Warren reexamined the transaction in the light of "looking intently" after the seller's interests as well as his own. After an intense inner struggle (and to the great surprise of the seller), he concluded that he should pay more for the property to reflect its true value. Practicing the Golden Rule is sometimes costly, but its reward is a clear conscience before God and other people.

2. MAINTAIN A HEALTHY FEAR OF THE LORD.

When we talk of a "healthy fear" of the Lord, we're not implying that God is a big bully just waiting for the opportunity to punish us. Far from it. In fact, He is a loving Father who, out of infinite love, disciplines His children for their benefit. *"He disciplines us for our good, so that we may share His holiness"* (Hebrews 12:10).

God uses this "healthy fear" to motivate us toward honesty in all our dealings. Proverbs 16:6 says, *"By the fear of the Lord one keeps away from evil."* Hebrews 12:11 warns us: *"All discipline for the moment seems not to be joyful, but sorrowful."* Discipline hurts! Given the choice, we should obey His Word rather than make a deliberate decision that will prompt our loving Father to discipline us.

We believe our heavenly Father will not allow us to keep anything we have acquired dishonestly. Proverbs 13:11 reads, *"Wealth obtained by fraud dwindles."*

A friend purchased four azalea plants, but the checkout clerk had only charged her for one. She knew it, but she left the store without paying for the other three. She told me it was miraculous how quickly three of those plants died!

Think about this: If you are a parent and your child steals something, do you allow the child to keep it? Of course not, because keeping it would damage the child's character. Not only do you insist on its return, but you usually want the child to experience enough discomfort to produce a lasting impression. For instance, you might have the child confess the theft to the store manager. When our heavenly Father lovingly disciplines us, He usually does it in a way we won't forget.

3. STAY AWAY FROM DISHONEST PEOPLE.

Scripture teaches that we are deeply influenced by those around us, either for good or for evil. Paul wrote, *"Do not be deceived: 'Bad company corrupts good morals'"* (1 Corinthians 15:33). Solomon was even stronger: *"He who is a partner with a thief hates his own life"* (Proverbs 29:24).

If I observe a person who is dishonest in dealing with the government or in a small matter, I know this person will be dishonest in greater matters—and probably in dealing with me. I believe it is impossible for people to be selectively honest. Either they have made the commitment to be completely honest or their dishonesty will become more prevalent. It's much easier to remain absolutely honest if you are surrounded by others who hold to that same conviction.

4. GIVE GENEROUSLY.

We can help escape the temptation of acting dishonestly by giving generously to those in need. *"He who steals must steal no longer; but rather he must labor, performing with his own hands what is good, so that he will have something to share with one who has need"* (Ephesians 4:28). Giving draws us closer to Christ, and reduces our incentive to steal. After all, if we're going to give something away, there's no reason to steal it!

WHAT TO DO WHEN DISHONEST

Unfortunately, we sometimes slip and act dishonestly. Once we recognize it, we need to do the following.

1. RESTORE OUR FELLOWSHIP WITH GOD.

Anytime we sin, we break fellowship with God and need to restore it. First John 1:9 tells us how: *"If we confess our sins, He is faithful and righteous to forgive us our sins and to cleanse us from all unrighteousness."* We must agree with God that our dishonesty was sin, and then thankfully accept His gracious forgiveness so we can again enjoy His fellowship. Remember, God loves us. He is kind and merciful, ready to forgive our dishonesty when we turn from it.

2. RESTORE OUR FELLOWSHIP WITH THE HARMED PERSON.

After our fellowship with God has been restored, we need to confess our dishonesty to the person we offended. *"Confess your sins to one another"* (James 5:16).

Ouch! This hurts. Only a handful of people have confessed wronging me. Interestingly, these people have become some of my closest friends. They so desired an honest relationship that they were willing to expose their sins.

Confessing has been very hard for me. My first experience came years ago when I went to someone I had wronged and confessed my sin—not that I hadn't had plenty of opportunities before! In the past, however, my pride had stood in the way. Afterward I sensed a great freedom in our relationship.

Failing to confess and restore fellowship may result in a lack of financial prosperity. *"He who con-*

ceals his transgressions will not prosper, but he who confesses and forsakes them will find compassion" (Proverbs 28:13).

3. RESTORE DISHONESTLY ACQUIRED PROPERTY.

If we have acquired anything dishonestly, we must return it to its rightful owner. *"Then it shall be, when he sins and becomes guilty, that he shall restore what he took by robbery…or anything about which he swore falsely; he shall make restitution for it in full and add to it one-fifth more. He shall give it to the one to whom it belongs"* (Leviticus 6:4-5).

Restitution is a tangible expression of repentance and an effort to correct a wrong. Zacchaeus is a good example. He promised Jesus, *"If I have defrauded anyone of anything, I will give back four times as much"* (Luke 19:8).

If it's not possible for restitution to be made, then the property should be given to the Lord. Numbers 5:8 teaches, *"If the man has no relative to whom restitution may be made for the wrong, the restitution which is made for the wrong must go to the Lord."*

HONESTY REQUIRED FOR LEADERS

The Lord is especially concerned with the honesty of leaders, because they influence those who follow them. The owner of a trucking business began wearing cowboy boots to work. Within six months, all the men in his office were in boots. He suddenly changed to traditional business shoes, and six months later, all the men were wearing business shoes.

In a similar way, a dishonest leader produces dishonest followers. *"If a ruler pays attention to falsehood, all his ministers become wicked"* (Proverbs 29:12). Leaders of a business, church, or home must set the example of honesty in their personal life before those under their authority can be expected to do the same.

SELECTION AND RETENTION OF LEADERS

Dishonesty should disqualify a person from leadership. Listen to the counsel of Jethro, Moses' father-in-law: *"You shall select out of all the people able men who fear God, men of truth, those who hate dishonest gain; and you shall place these…as leaders of thousands, of hundreds, of fifties and of tens"* (Exodus 18:21). Two of the four criteria for leadership selection dealt with honesty: *"men of truth, those who hate dishonest gain."*

Not only are leaders selected in part by honest behavior, but a leader retains this position by acting honestly. *"A leader…who hates unjust gain will prolong his days"* (Proverbs 28:16). We have all witnessed leaders in business or government who have been removed because of personal corruption.

How can a leader maintain absolute honesty? By becoming accountable to others. It's necessary to establish a system of checks and balances that do not usurp the leader's authority, but provide a structure to ensure accountability.

BRIBES

A bribe is anything given to influence a person to do something illegal or wrong. The taking of bribes is clearly prohibited in the Bible: *"You shall not take a bribe, for a bribe blinds the clear-sighted and subverts the cause of the just"* (Exodus 23:8). Bribes frequently come packaged as "gifts" or "referral fees." Evaluate any such offer to confirm that it is not a bribe in disguise. If you have any doubts or discomfort, politely refuse to receive any such benefit.

BLESSINGS AND CURSES

Listed below are some of the blessings the Lord has promised for the honest—and some of the curses reserved for the dishonest. Read these slowly, asking God to use them to motivate you to a life of honesty.

BLESSINGS FOR THE HONEST

- Blessing of a more intimate relationship with the Lord. *"For the crooked man is an abomination to the LORD; but He is intimate with the upright"* (Proverbs 3:32).
- Blessings on the family. *"A righteous man who walks in his integrity—how blessed are his sons after him"* (Proverbs 20:7).
- Blessings of life. *"Truthful lips will be established forever, but a lying tongue is only for a moment"* (Proverbs 12:19).
- Blessings of prosperity. *"Much wealth is in the house of the righteous, but trouble is in the income of the wicked"* (Proverbs 15:6).

CURSES RESERVED FOR THE DISHONEST

- Curse of alienation from God. *"For the crooked man is an abomination to the LORD"* (Proverbs 3:32).
- Curse on the family. *"He who profits illicitly troubles his own house, but he who hates bribes will live"* (Proverbs 15:27).
- Curse of death. *"The getting of treasures by a lying tongue is a fleeting vapor, the pursuit of death"* (Proverbs 21:6).
- Curse of poverty. *"Wealth obtained by fraud dwindles"* (Proverbs 13:11).

COUNSEL

Sometimes when I counsel people with deep financial problems, I am saddened. I know that if only these individuals would have sought counsel early-on from someone with a solid understanding of God's way of handling money, they would have avoided untold pain and heartache.

Two attitudes keep us from seeking counsel. The first is *pride*. Our culture regards seeking advice as a sign of weakness. The second attitude is *stubbornness*, characterized by the statement, "Don't confuse me with the facts. My mind is already made up!" We often resist seeking counsel because we don't want to be told we can't afford what we already have decided to buy.

God encourages us to use a gift He has provided for our benefit—godly counselors. In Proverbs 19:20 we read, *"Listen to advice and accept instruction, and in the end you will be wise"* (NIV).

Proverbs 12:15 says, *"The way of a fool is right in his own eyes, but a wise man is he who listens to counsel."*

And Proverbs 10:8 says, *"The wise man is glad to be instructed, but a self-sufficient fool falls flat on his face"* (TLB).

We seek counsel to secure insights, suggestions, and alternatives that will aid in making a proper decision. It's not, however, the counselor's role to make the decision; we retain that responsibility.

Gather facts, but....

We need to assemble the facts that will influence our decisions, but we also need to seek God's direction as well. What we have to remember is that He will sometimes direct us in a way contrary to our assessment of the facts alone.

We can see this illustrated in the chapters of Numbers 13 and 14. Moses sent twelve spies into the Promised Land, and they all returned with an identical evaluation of the facts: It was a prosperous land inhabited by terrifying giants. Only two of the twelve spies, Joshua and Caleb, understood that the Lord wanted them to go in and possess the Promised Land anyway—in spite of the obstacles! Because the children of Israel relied only on the facts, and did not act in faith on what the Lord wanted for them, they suffered 40 years of wandering in the wilderness, until that entire generation died.

SOURCES OF COUNSEL

What are the sources of counsel we need to seek? Before making a financial decision, particularly an important one, subject it to three sources of counsel.

THE BIBLE

First, what does God's Word say about an issue? The psalmist wrote, *"Your laws are both my light and my counselors"* (Psalm 119:24, TLB). *"Your commands make me wiser than my enemies.... I have more insight than all my teachers, for I meditate on your statutes"* (Psalm 119:98-99, NIV). *"I understand more than the aged, because I have observed Your precepts"* (Psalm 119:100).

When we think of people who are skilled in financial decision making, we often think of experts, or those who are older and more experienced. Yet the Bible offers us more insight and wisdom than financial experts who don't know God's way of handling money. I would rather obey the truth of Scripture than risk suffering the consequences of following my own inclinations or the opinions of so-called experts.

The Bible makes this remarkable claim about itself: *"For the word of God is living and active and sharper than any two-edged sword, and...able to judge the thoughts and intentions of the heart"* (Hebrews 4:12). The truths in the Bible are timeless. It is truly a living book that communicates God's direction to all generations.

You may have been surprised to learn that the Bible contains 2,350 verses dealing with how we should handle money. The fact is, the Scriptures are the very first filter through which we should run our financial decisions. If the Bible answers the question, we don't have to go any further, because it contains the Lord's written, revealed will.

Bob and Barbara faced a difficult choice. Barbara's brother and his wife had just moved to Florida. Because they had previously experienced financial difficulties, the bank would not give them a home loan unless they had someone cosign it. They asked Bob and Barbara, and although Barbara pleaded for Bob to cosign, he was reluctant.

A friend referred them to the verses that warn against cosigning. After reading the passages, Barbara said, "Who am I to argue with God? We shouldn't cosign." Bob was tremendously relieved.

Two years later, Barbara's brother and his wife were divorced, and he declared bankruptcy. Can you imagine the strain on their marriage if Bob had cosigned? He might have said, "Barbara, you got me into this! I tried not to cosign, but you forced me!" They probably would not have been able to survive financially.

If the Bible provides clear direction in a financial matter, we know what to do. If the Bible is not specific about an issue, we should subject our decision to the second source of counsel: godly people.

GODLY PEOPLE

"The godly man is a good counselor because he is just and fair and knows right from wrong" (Psalm 37:30-31, TLB).

Spouse

If you are married, the first person you need to consult is your spouse. Frankly, it has been a humbling experience for me to seek the counsel of my wife, Bev, in financial matters because she has no formal financial training. Even so, she has saved us tons of money by her wise counsel.

Women tend to be gifted with a wonderfully sensitive intuition that is usually very accurate. Men tend to focus more objectively on the facts. The husband and wife need each other to achieve the proper balance for a correct decision. I believe that the Lord honors the wife's "office" as helper to her husband. Many times the Lord communicates most clearly to the husband through his wife.

If you are a husband, let me be blunt. Regardless of her business background or her financial aptitude, *you must cultivate and seek your wife's counsel.* I have committed never to proceed with a financial decision unless Bev agrees.

The husband and wife should agree because they both will experience the consequences of the decision. Even if their choice proves to be disastrous, there are no grounds for an "I told you so" fracture in their relationship. There are other benefits of seeking such counsel as well.

It honors your spouse. Unfortunately, some in our culture don't feel valuable. Seeking your spouse's counsel will help enormously in the development of a healthy self-esteem. When a husband or wife seeks the other's advice, he or she actually is communicating, "I love you. I respect you. I value your insight."

It prepares your spouse for the future. Consistently asking for advice also keeps your spouse informed of your financial condition. This is important in the event you predecease your spouse or are unable to work. My father suffered a heart attack that incapacitated him for two years. But because he had kept my mother informed about his business, she was able to step in and operate it until he recovered.

Parents

Our parents are a source of counsel. *"My son, observe the commandment of your father and do not forsake the teaching of your mother; bind them continually on your heart; tie them around your neck. When you walk about, they will guide you; when you sleep, they will watch over you; and when you awake, they will talk to you"* (Proverbs 6:20-22).

Our parents have the benefit of years of experience, and they know us well. In our opinion, we should seek their counsel even if they don't yet know Christ or have not been wise money managers themselves. Asking their advice is a way to honor our parents and to build a closer relationship with them. It's an expression of admiration.

One word of caution, however. Although the husband and wife should seek the counsel of their parents, the advice of the parents should be subordinate to the advice of the spouse—especially if a family conflict materializes. *"A man shall leave his father and his mother, and shall be joined to his wife; and they shall become one flesh"* (Genesis 2:24, NIV).

Experienced people

We should also consult people experienced in the area in which we are attempting to make a decision. If you are considering a real estate investment, locate the most qualified real estate investor to counsel you.

A multitude of counselors

We read in Proverbs 15:22, *"Without consultation, plans are frustrated, but with many counselors they succeed."* And Proverbs 11:14 says, *"Where there is no guidance the people fall, but in abundance of counselors there is victory."*

I meet regularly with a small group. The members of this group know each other well. Over the years, each person has experienced a difficult circumstance. We have learned that when someone suffers a painful situation, it can be difficult to make wise decisions. We have experienced the safety of having a group who love one another and can give objective counsel—even if it hurts. We are more receptive to constructive criticism when it comes from someone who cares for us.

Solomon describes the benefits of dependence upon one another:

"Two are better than one because they have a good return for their labor. For if either of them falls, the one will lift up his companion. But woe to the one who falls when there is not another to lift him up... And if one can overpower him who is alone, two can resist him. A cord of three strands is not quickly torn apart" (Ecclesiastes 4:9-12).

When seeking a multitude of counselors, don't expect them all to offer the same recommendations. They may even disagree sharply, but a common thread usually develops. At other times, each counselor may supply a different insight you need to help you make the decision. We encourage you to include your pastor among your counselors, particularly when you face a major crossroads.

THE LORD

During the process of analyzing the facts, searching the Bible, and obtaining the counsel of godly people, we need to seek direction from the Lord. In fact, this is the most important thing we can do. In Isaiah 9:6, we are told that one of the Lord's names is *"Wonderful Counselor."*

The Psalms also identify the Lord as our counselor. *"I* [the Lord] *will instruct you and teach you in the way which you should go; I will counsel you with My eye upon you"* (Psalm 32:8). *"You* [the Lord] *guide me with your counsel"* (Psalm 73:24, NIV).

The Bible contains numerous examples of the unfortunate consequences of not seeking God's counsel, as well as the blessings of heeding His counsel. After the children of Israel began their campaign to capture the Promised Land, some of the natives (Gibeonites) attempted to enter into a peace treaty with Israel. The Gibeonites deceived the leaders of Israel into believing they were from a distant land. Joshua 9:14-15 reads, *"The men of Israel took some of their* [Gibeonites'] *provisions, and* ***did not ask for the counsel of the Lord****. Joshua made peace with them and made a covenant with them, to let them live"* (emphasis added).

The consequence of not seeking the Lord's counsel was that the Promised Land remained populated with ungodly people, and Israel became ensnared by their false gods. The leaders were influenced by the "facts" they could see—facts deliberately designed to deceive them into thinking that the Gibeonites lived far away. In many situations, only the Lord can reveal truth and proper direction.

Throughout Scripture we are encouraged to wait on the Lord. Whenever you feel hurried or pressured or confused concerning a decision, wait until you hear His still, small voice. The world screams "Hurry!" but our heavenly Father's advice is worth waiting for...a thousand times over.

COUNSEL TO AVOID

THE WICKED

We need to avoid the counsel of the wicked. *"How blessed is the man who does not walk in the counsel of the wicked"* (Psalm 1:1). A "wicked" person is one who lives without regard to God. A wicked person can be one who does not yet personally know the Lord or one who knows Jesus Christ as Savior, but is not following Him in obedience.

In our opinion, when you are searching for facts or technical expertise, you may seek input from those who are knowledgeable in that area, whether they know Christ or not. Then, after considering their input, you are responsible to make the final decision.

FORTUNETELLERS, MEDIUMS AND SPIRITUALISTS

The Bible clearly forbids seeking the advice of fortunetellers, mediums, or spiritualists: *"Do not turn to mediums or seek out spiritists, for you will be defiled by them. I am the Lord your God"* (Leviticus 19:31, NIV). Or consider this passage: *"Saul died because he was unfaithful to the Lord…and even consulted a medium for guidance and did not inquire of the Lord. So the Lord put him to death"* (1 Chronicles 10:13-14, NIV). Saul died, in part, because he went to a medium. We should also avoid anything they use in forecasting the future, such as horoscopes and all other practices of the occult.

BIASED COUNSEL

We need to be cautious of the counsel of the biased. When receiving financial advice, ask yourself: "What stake does this person have in the outcome of my decision? Does he or she stand to gain or lose from it?" If the advisor will profit, always seek a second, unbiased opinion.

A WORD TO THE COUNSELED

When you are seeking advice, supply your counselor with all the important facts. Don't attempt to manipulate your advisor to give the answer you want by concealing information.

Whenever you face a major decision, such as a job change or home purchase, it is very helpful to go to a quiet place where you can spend uninterrupted time praying, reading the Bible, and seeking the Lord's direction. We encourage you to consider fasting during this time.

As you seek counsel, don't be surprised if the answer comes out of your own mouth! Interacting with others allows you to verbalize thoughts and feelings that you may never have expressed clearly.

A WORD TO COUNSELORS

Counseling others can be frustrating if you misunderstand the proper role of the counselor. Simply stated, counselors should lovingly communicate their advice—and then leave the results to God. I have made the mistake of becoming involved emotionally in whether people would act on my recommendations. I discovered that some people aren't yet prepared to follow advice. It may have been the right word for them, but in the wrong season of their lives. On other occasions, I later discovered that my counsel was flawed, and I was happy that they hadn't heeded my words!

When you don't know the answer to a question, be careful not to fabricate one. Simply respond: "I don't know." Often people come with problems that are outside of our experience. The best way to serve them is to refer them to someone who has expertise in their area of need.

LET'S GET PRACTICAL!

THE FILING SYSTEM

It is important to keep invoices, checks, statements and receipts that are necessary for your income tax records or are the only evidence of a paid bill. Bev and I have benefited from a simple filing system dozens of times. It requires an average of less than one minute a day, and can save you hours of searching. We suggest you keep the receipts for seven years before destroying them.

You can choose one of several methods of filing:

1. **Save and File Hard Copies.** File them in a shoebox, using a separate box for each year. Simple dividers are adequate with the following headings: Income, Giving, Medical, Business Expenses, Insurance, Interest, Taxes, Auto, Utilities, Telephone, Home Improvements, Credit Card Statements, and Bank Statements. Add or delete categories, depending on your personal needs.
2. **Scan and Save Electronic Files.** If you have the ability to scan documents, you may choose to scan your receipts and statements electronically. Create a folder for each year and then save to your computer. It's wise to back up these documents on an external hard drive. If you can't scan documents, some office stores can perform this service.
3. **Scan and Save Online.** A third option is to save scanned documents online. There are companies that provide secure, password protected online file storage.

DETERMINING YOUR LIFE INSURANCE NEEDS

Complete the Life Insurance Worksheet to approximate your life insurance needs. This is not intended to be precise. Seek the counsel of an expert to determine your needs accurately.

Your **Annual income needs** figure should represent your household's income needs. Then, **subtract the deceased person's living expenses** that will no longer be needed if a breadwinner passes away, such as, income taxes reduced and less food consumed. Also **subtract other income** survivors will receive from all sources, such as Social Security, investments, and the surviving spouse's earnings. This calculation will give you the **net income needed** for the survivors to maintain their current standard of living.

To estimate the amount of **insurance you will need for income,** multiply the income required by 20. This assumes the survivors will earn a 5 percent return, after taxes, on the insurance proceeds.

Insurance coverage may also be needed to fund **"lump sums,"** such as, paying off debt or funding a child's education. Determine these needs and add them to the total amount of the insurance.

Keep in mind that your personal figures can be broad estimates that can be used to start a conversation with an insurance professional. Most participants in the small group study will be surprised to learn how much insurance is needed to cover a breadwinner's lost income.

LIFE INSURANCE WORKSHEET

Sample annual income needs	\$58,000
Subtract deceased person's needs	\$10,000
Subtract other income	\$12,000
= Net annual income needed	\$36,000
Net annual income needed, multiplied by 20 (assumes 5% after-tax investment return on insurance proceeds)	\$720,000
Lump Sum Needs	
Debts	\$12,000
Education	\$15,000
Other	\$ 0
Total lump sum needs	\$27,000
Total life insurance needs	\$747,000

SAMPLE

LIFE INSURANCE WORKSHEET

Your annual income needs $______________

Subtract deceased person's needs $______________

Subtract other income $______________

= Net annual income needed $______________

Net annual income needed, multiplied by 20 (assumes 5% after-tax investment return on insurance proceeds) $______________

Lump Sum Needs

Debts $______________

Education $______________

Other $______________

Total lump sum needs $______________

Total life insurance needs $______________

5

GENEROSITY

FACILITATORS GUIDE

"Remember the words of the Lord Jesus, that He Himself said, 'It is more blessed to give than to receive'" (Acts 20:35).

GENEROSITY

Facilitators Guide for Week 5

Overview: Emphasize the importance of giving with the proper attitude.

Let's Get Practical!

☐ Continue **Recording your Income and Spending** on pages 44-45 if you are using a Compass budget. **If you're using the online Money Lounge™ budget**, log on to www.compass1.org, click on Small Group Studies Tools & Resources and then click on the Navigating Study Student and Facilitator Tools.

☐ Complete your **Journey to Generosity** on pages 126-127.

Agenda

1.__________ (5 minutes) Open in prayer.

2.__________ (5 minutes) Each individual recites from memory:

"Remember the words of the Lord Jesus, that He Himself said, 'It is more blessed to give than to receive'" (Acts 20:35).

3.__________ (85 minutes) Begin the group discussion.

Day One (Giving Attitudes)

Complete the Journey to Generosity on pages 126-127.

1. Do you have any questions about the Journey to Generosity?

2. What did you learn from completing it that will improve your giving?

Read *Matthew 23:23; 1 Corinthians 13:3* and *2 Corinthians 9:7.*

3. What do these passages communicate about the importance of the proper attitude in giving?

Matthew 23:23— [The Pharisees gave exactly the correct amount—even a tithe of their mint leaves. However, because they gave with the wrong attitude, the Lord rebuked them.]

1 Corinthians 13:3— [Giving without love is of no value to the giver.]

2 Corinthians 9:7— [The proper attitude is the key issue in giving. The only way to give out of a heart of love is to consciously give each gift to Jesus Christ as an act of worship.]

4. How would you describe your attitude in giving, and how do you think you can improve it if it needs to be adjusted?

Day Two (Benefits of Generosity)

Read *Acts 20:35*.

1. How does this principle from God's economy differ from the way most people view giving?

[In God's economic system, it is more blessed to give than to receive. Most people believe the opposite.]

2. Identify the benefits for the giver in the following passages and describe how they might encourage you to be more generous.

Proverbs 11:24-25— [There is a material increase—in the Lord's time and way—to the giver.]

Matthew 6:20— [We can lay up treasures in heaven that we will be able to enjoy throughout all eternity.]

Luke 12:34— [The heart of the giver is drawn to Christ as treasures are given to Him.]

1 Timothy 6:18-19—- [We can store treasures in heaven, and while on earth we can "take hold of that which is life indeed."]

Day Three (Amount to Give)

Read *Malachi 3:8-10.*

1. What was God's view on tithing (giving 10 percent) in the Old Testament, and how has that impacted your generosity?

[The tithe was required under the law, and it was considered robbing God not to give these required gifts.]

Read *2 Corinthians 8:1-5.*

2. Identify three principles from this passage that might influence how much you give.

[This passage focuses on the churches of Macedonia, who experienced difficult circumstances (*"a great ordeal of affliction"* and *"deep poverty"*) but gave generously (*"beyond their ability"*) and cheerfully (*"abundance of joy"*).]

- [They first gave themselves to the Lord, asking Him to direct their giving. In a similar way, we should yield ourselves to God when determining how much to give.]
- [They were so submitted to the Lord that despite terrible circumstances they begged to give.]
- [They experienced joy as a result of their sacrificial giving.]

Prayerfully (with your spouse if you are married) seek the Lord's guidance to determine how much you should give. You will not be asked to disclose the amount.

* *Facilitator*, you should have about **one hour** of class time remaining.

Day Four (Where to Give)

Read *Numbers 18:8-10, 24; Galatians 6:6* and *1 Timothy 5:17-18.*

1. What do these verses say about financially supporting your church and those who teach the Bible? How do you plan on practicing this?

Numbers 18:8-10, 24— [God's people have always been required to fund ministry. The Old Testament believer was required to care for the place of worship and the Levites who served in the ministry.]

Galatians 6:6— [Those who are taught the Bible should financially support their teachers.]

1 Timothy 5:17-18— [God's New Testament instrument is the church, and we are to adequately support those who serve as pastors and teachers.]

Day Five (Giving to the Poor and Needy)

Read *Isaiah 58:6-11* and *Ezekiel 16:49*.

1. What do these verses say to you about giving to the poor?

Isaiah 58:6-11— [When we give to the poor, the Lord will protect us, answer our prayers, and bless us with His joy.]

Ezekiel 16:49— [The primary sins of Sodom were pride and not caring for the poor, even though they had an abundance of material goods.]

Read *Matthew 25:35-45.*

2. How does Jesus Christ identify with the needy and how does this impact your thinking?

[Jesus identifies personally with the poor. When we give to the poor, we are giving to Christ Himself. When we do not give to the poor, we are not giving to Christ, and He is left hungry and naked.]

Read *Galatians 2:9-10.*

3. What does this verse communicate to you about giving to the poor?

[The disciples had a deep concern for the poor. After Paul's confirmation to minister to the Gentiles, the only counsel the disciples gave him was not to forget the poor. Think of the many issues they could have discussed. Yet, they only asked Paul to remember the poor.]

4. Are you currently giving to the needy? If not, what is hindering you?

Day Six (the Notes)

Read the Generosity Notes on pages 117-125.

1. What truth about giving did you learn that proved especially helpful? In what way?

2. What principle of generosity will you apply after reading the Notes?

3. I'll take the following *action* as a result of this week's study.

Remaining Agenda

1. __________ (10 minutes) Play the Week 5 segment of the *Navigating Your Finances* DVD.
2. __________ (10 minutes) Note in the Prayer Log requests and answers to prayers.
3. __________ (5 minutes) End in prayer.

GENEROSITY NOTES

Please read *after* completing Day 5 homework.

Few areas of the Christian life can be more misunderstood and frustrating than that of generosity. For several years after I met Christ, I did my best to avoid giving. On those occasions when I felt obligated to give in order to appear spiritual, I did so, but my heart wasn't in it.

My whole perspective changed after learning what the Bible actually teaches. Suddenly I *wanted* to be generous. But then I was frustrated by another problem: an unlimited number of needs versus my limited resources. How should I decide where to give? My church, the hungry poor, campus and prison ministries, missionary efforts, radio and television programs, and many other vital ministries needed financial support.

Intense competition for resources makes these decisions even more difficult. It seems as if my mailbox is constantly full of appeals. I react to these requests with mixed emotions: compassion, gratitude, guilt, and even cynicism. I feel deep compassion and almost despair when confronted with those facing starvation of body or spirit. I am grateful for the people dedicated to meet those needs, and feel guilty that perhaps we aren't giving enough. At other times, however, I feel cynical about being solicited—and perhaps manipulated—by people whose goals may be worthwhile, but whose methods are questionable.

We will examine four elements of giving: attitudes, advantages, amount, and approach.

ATTITUDES IN GIVING

God evaluates our actions on the basis of our attitudes. John 3:16 reveals His attitude toward giving: *"For God so **loved** the world, that He **gave** His only begotten Son"* (emphasis added). Note the sequence. Because God loved, He gave. Because God is love, He is also a giver. He set the example of generosity motivated by love.

An attitude of love in giving is crucial: *"If I give all my possessions to feed the poor... but do not have love, it profits me nothing"* (1 Corinthians 13:3).

What could be more commendable than giving everything to the poor? However, generosity without an attitude of love provides no benefit to the giver.

In God's economy, the attitude is more important than the amount. Jesus emphasized this in Matthew 23:23: *"Woe to you, teachers of the law and Pharisees, you hypocrites! You give a tenth of your spices—mint, dill and cummin. But you have neglected the more important matters of the law—justice, mercy and faithfulness. You should have practiced the latter without neglecting the former"* (NIV). The Pharisees had been careful to give the correct amount, but Christ rebuked them because of their attitude. He looks past the amount of the gift to the heart of the giver.

We can consistently give with love only when we recognize that we are giving to the Lord Himself. We see an example of this in Numbers 18:24: *"The tithe of the sons of Israel... they offer as an offering **to the Lord"*** (emphasis added). If giving is merely to a church, a ministry, or a needy person, it's only charity. But giving to the Lord is always an act of worship, expressing love and gratitude to our Creator, Savior, and faithful Provider. Whenever we put something in the offering plate, we should remind ourselves that our gift goes to the Lord Himself.

In addition to giving with love, we are to give cheerfully. *"Each one must do just as he has purposed in his heart, not grudgingly or under compulsion, for God loves a cheerful giver"* (2 Corinthians 9:7). The original Greek word for cheerful is hilarios, which is translated into the English word hilarious. What a picture that creates! We are to be joyful givers.

When was the last time you saw hilarity when the offering plate passed? The atmosphere more often reminds us of a patient in the dentist chair awaiting a painful extraction. So how do we develop this hilarity in our giving? Consider the early churches of Macedonia.

"We want you to know about the grace that God has given the Macedonian churches. Out of the most severe trial, their overflowing joy and their extreme poverty welled up in rich generosity" (2 Corinthians 8:1-2, NIV).

How did the Macedonians, who were in terrible circumstances, "severe trial," and "extreme poverty," still manage to give with "overflowing joy"? The answer is in verse 5: *"They gave themselves first to the Lord and then to us in keeping with God's will."* The key to cheerful giving is to yield ourselves to Christ, and ask Him to direct how much He wants us to give. That places us in a position to experience the advantages of giving with the proper attitude.

Stop and examine yourself. What is your attitude toward giving?

ADVANTAGES OF GIVING

Gifts obviously benefit the recipient. The church continues its ministry, the hungry are fed, the naked are clothed, and missionaries are sent. But in God's economy, gifts given with the proper attitude benefit the giver more than the receiver. *"Remember the words of the Lord Jesus, that He Himself said, 'It is more blessed to give than to receive'"* (Acts 20:35). As we examine Scripture, we find that the giver benefits in four significant areas.

1. An increase in intimacy

Above all else, giving directs our hearts to Christ. Matthew 6:21 tells us, *"For where your treasure is, there your heart will be also."* This is why it's necessary to give each gift to the person of Jesus Christ: it draws our hearts to Him.

Do you remember the faithful steward in the parable of the talents, and his eventual reward? *"Enter into the joy of your Master"* (Matthew 25:21). Giving is one of your responsibilities as a steward, and the more faithful you are in fulfilling your responsibilities, the more you can enter into the joy of knowing Christ more closely. Nothing in life compares with that.

2. An increase in character

Our heavenly Father wants us—His children—to conform to the image of His Son. The character of Christ is that of an unselfish giver. Unfortunately, humans are selfish by nature. One essential way we become conformed to Christ is by regular giving. Someone once said, "Giving is not God's way of raising money; it is God's way of raising people into the likeness of His Son."

3. An increase in heaven

Matthew 6:20 reads, *"Store up for yourselves treasures in heaven, where neither moth nor rust destroys, and where thieves do not break in or steal."* The Lord tells us that heaven has its own "First National Bank," where we can invest for eternity.

Paul wrote, *"Not that I seek the gift itself, but I seek for the profit which increases to your account"* (Philippians 4:17). Each of us has an account in heaven that we will be able to enjoy for eternity. And although it's true that we "can't take it with us when we die," Scripture teaches that we can make deposits to our heavenly account before we die.

4. An increase on earth

Many people have a hard time believing that giving results in material blessings flowing back to the giver. Time and again, however, we encounter that very truth in the pages of Scripture.

Consider Proverbs 11:24-25: *"There is one who scatters, and yet increases all the more, and there is one who withholds what is justly due, and yet it results only in want. The generous man will be prosperous, and he who waters will himself be watered."*

Examine 2 Corinthians 9:6-11: *"He who sows sparingly will also reap sparingly, and he who sows bountifully will also reap bountifully.... God is able to make all grace abound to you, so that always having all sufficiency in everything, you may have an abundance for every good deed.... Now He who supplies seed to the sower and bread for food will supply and multiply your seed for sowing and increase the harvest of your righteousness; you will be enriched in everything for all liberality."*

These verses clearly teach that giving results in a material increase: *"will also reap bountifully ... always having all sufficiency in everything...may have an abundance...will supply and multiply your seed... you will be enriched in everything."*

But note carefully **why** the Lord returns a material increase: *"Always having all sufficiency in everything, you may have an abundance for every good deed...will supply and multiply your seed for sowing... you will be enriched in everything for all liberality."* As shown in the diagram below, the Lord produces an increase so that we may give more and have our needs met at the same time.

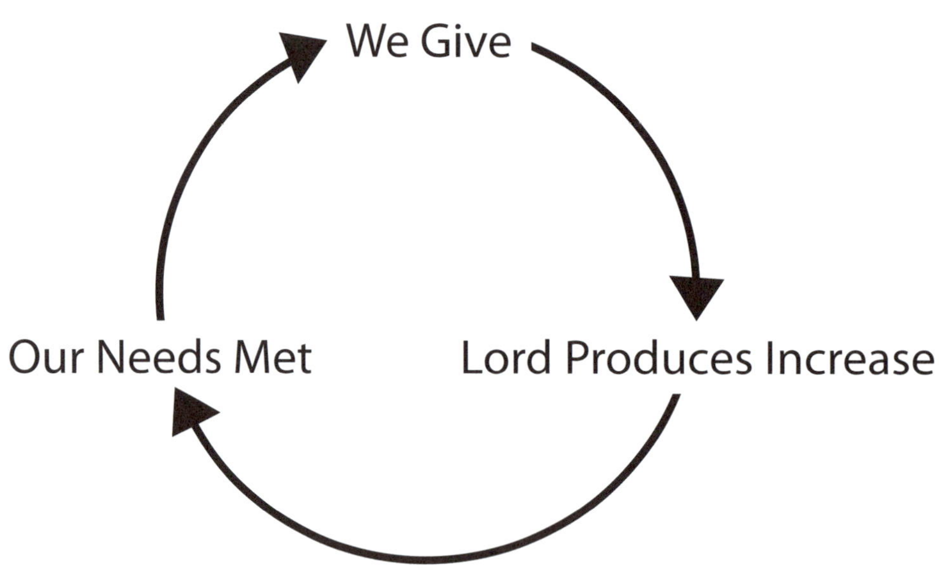

Study the cycle of giving. One reason the Lord reveals that we can anticipate a material increase is because He wants us to recognize that He is behind it. God has chosen to be invisible, but He wants us to experience His reality.

When we give, we should do so with a sense of expectation—anticipating an increase from the

Lord, even though we have no idea how or when He may choose to provide it. Our experience has shown Him to be very creative! Remember, givers experience the advantages of giving only when they give cheerfully and with love—not when the motive is just to get.

AMOUNT TO GIVE

Let's survey what the Bible says about how much to give. Before the Old Testament Law, there were two instances of giving a known amount. In Genesis 14:20, Abraham gave 10 percent—a tithe—after the rescue of his nephew Lot. And in Genesis 28:22, Jacob promised to give the Lord a tenth of all his possessions if God brought him safely through his journey.

With the Law came the requirement of the tithe. The Lord condemns the children of Israel in Malachi 3:8-9 for not tithing properly: *"Will a man rob God? Yet you are robbing Me! But you say, 'How have we robbed You?' In tithes and offerings. You are cursed with a curse, for you are robbing Me, the whole nation of you!"*

In addition to the tithe, there were various offerings. The Lord also made special provisions for the poor. Every seven years all debts were forgiven; every 50 years, the land was returned to the original land-owning families. Special harvesting rules allowed the poor to glean behind the harvesters.

God made another significant provision for the poor in Deuteronomy 15:7-8: *"If there is a poor man with you, one of your brothers, in any of your towns in your land which the Lord your God is giving you, you shall not harden your heart, nor close your hand from your poor brother; but you shall freely open your hand to him, and shall generously lend him sufficient for his need in whatever he lacks."* Even under the law, the extent of one's giving was not to be limited by a locked-in fixed percentage, but was to be adjusted by surrounding needs.

The New Testament teaches that we are to give in proportion to the material blessing we receive. It also commends sacrificial giving.

What I like about the tithe is that it's systematic, and the amount of the gift is easy to compute. The danger of the tithe is that it can be treated as simply "another bill" to be paid. If we fall into that sort of attitude or rut, we won't be in a position to receive God's richest blessings. Another potential danger of tithing is the assumption that once we have tithed, we have fulfilled all our obligations to give. For many Christians, the tithe should be the *beginning* of their giving, not the limit. And we should never, never close our hearts to the obvious needs we encounter in our path through life.

How much should you give? To answer this question, first give yourself to the Lord. Submit yourself to Him. Earnestly seek His will for you concerning giving. Ask Him to help you obey Christ's leading. We are convinced that we should tithe as a minimum, and then give over and above the tithe as the Lord prospers or directs us.

APPROACH TO GIVING

During Paul's third missionary journey, one of his priorities was to take up a collection for the suffering believers in Jerusalem. We draw several practical applications from his instructions concerning this collection. *"On the first day of every week each one of you is to put aside and save, as he may prosper, so that no collections be made when I come"* (1 Corinthians 16:2).

1. Giving should be periodic.

"On the first day of every week…." The Lord understands that we need to give frequently. Giving only once a year is a mistake. We need to give regularly to be drawn consistently to Christ.

2. Giving should be personal.

"Each one of you is to…." It is the responsibility of every child of God, whether young or old, rich or poor, to give. The advantages of giving are intended for each person, and each one must participate to enjoy them to the full.

3. Giving should be out of a private deposit.

"Put aside and save…." If you experience difficulty in monitoring the money you have decided to give, consider opening a separate account or setting aside a special "cookie jar" into which you deposit the money you intend to give. Then, as needs are brought to your attention, the money is ready to meet those needs.

4. Giving should be a priority.

"Honor the Lord from your wealth and from the first of all your produce" (Proverbs 3:9). As soon as we receive any income, we should set aside the amount we are going to give. This habit helps us to put Christ first in all we do—and defeats the temptation to spend what we have decided to give.

5. Giving should be premeditated.

"Each one must do just as he has purposed in his heart" (2 Corinthians 9:7). We should give prayerfully, exercising the same care in selecting where we give as we do when deciding where to invest.

6. Giving should be without pride.

To experience any of the Lord's benefits, don't ever give to impress people. Matthew 6:1-4 says, *"Be careful not to do your 'acts of righteousness' before men, to be seen by them. If you do, you will have no reward from your Father in heaven. So when you give to the needy, do not announce it with trumpets, as the hypocrites do in the synagogues and on the streets, to be honored by men.... They have received their reward in full. But when you give to the needy, do not let your left hand know what your right hand is doing, so that your giving may be in secret. Then your Father, who sees what is done in secret, will reward you"* (NIV).

PLACES FOR GIVING

In the Bible, we are instructed to give to three areas: the local church, ministries, and the poor and needy.

1. Giving to the local church and Christian ministries

Throughout its pages the Bible focuses on funding the ministry. The Old Testament priesthood received specific support: *"To the sons of Levi, behold, I have given all the tithe in Israel...in return for their service which they perform"* (Numbers 18:21). And New Testament teaching on ministerial support is just as strong. Unfortunately, some have wrongly taught poverty for Christian workers, influencing many to believe that everyone in Christian ministry should be poor. That position simply isn't scriptural. Listen to Paul's words to Timothy: *"Pastors who do their work well should be paid well and should be highly appreciated, especially those who work hard at both preaching and teaching"* (1 Timothy 5:17, TLB).

Over the years, we have seen how many Christian workers have actually been distracted from their ministry and rendered less effective because of their inadequate support. As someone has said, "The poor and starving pastor should exist only among poor and starving people."

People ask us if we give only through our church. In our case, the answer is no. However, giving to the local church should be a priority as a tangible expression of our commitment to it. But we also give to others who directly impact us. *"The one who is taught the word is to share all good things with the one who teaches"* (Galatians 6:6).

2. Giving to the poor

Matthew 25:34-45 teaches one of the most exciting and yet sobering truths in the Bible. Read this passage carefully.

> *"The King will say... 'For I was hungry and you gave Me something to eat; I was thirsty, and you gave Me something to drink.' ... Then the righteous will answer Him, 'Lord, when did we see You hungry, and feed You, or thirsty, and give You something to drink?' ... The King will answer and say to them.... 'To the extent that you did it to one of these brothers of Mine, even the least of them, you did it to Me.'*
>
> *"Then He will also say to those on His left, 'Depart from Me, accursed ones, into the eternal fire...*

for I was hungry, and you gave Me nothing to eat; I was thirsty, and you gave Me nothing to drink.... To the extent that you did not do it to one of the least of these, you did not do it to Me.'"

In a mysterious way we cannot fully understand, Jesus, the Creator of all things, personally identifies Himself with the poor. When we share with the needy, we are actually sharing with Jesus Himself. If that truth is staggering, then this is terrifying: When we do not give to the needy, we leave Christ Himself hungry and thirsty.

During Christ's earthly ministry, He consistently gave to the poor. When Jesus told Judas to go and carry out the betrayal during the Last Supper, *"no one of those reclining at the table knew for what purpose He had said this to him. For some were supposing, because Judas had the money box, that Jesus was saying to him, 'Buy things we have need of for the feast'; or else, that he should give something to the poor"* (John 13:28-29).

Giving to the needy was such a consistent part of Jesus' life that the disciples assumed He was sending Judas either to buy needed food or to give to the poor; no other alternative entered their minds.

After Paul met with the disciples to announce his ministry to the Gentiles, he said, *"They* [the disciples] *only asked us to remember the poor—the very thing I also was eager to do"* (Galatians 2:10). Think of all the issues the disciples could have discussed with Paul. But the only request they made was to remember the poor. Now that should tell us something!

Three areas of our Christian life are affected by whether we give to the poor.

Prayer

A lack of giving to the poor could be a source of unanswered prayer. *"Is this not the fast which I choose... to divide your bread with the hungry and bring the homeless poor into the house?... Then you will call and the LORD will answer"* (Isaiah 58:6-9). *"He who shuts his ear to the cry of the poor will also cry himself and not be answered"* (Proverbs 21:13).

Provision

Our giving to the needy may determine our provision. *"He who gives to the poor will never want, but he who shuts his eyes will have many curses"* (Proverbs 28:27).

Knowing Jesus Christ intimately

Those who refuse or neglect to share resources with the poor don't know the Lord as intimately as they could. *"'He pled the cause of the afflicted and the needy; then it was well. Is that not what it means to know Me?' declares the LORD"* (Jeremiah 22:16).

Giving to the poor has been discouraged, in part, because of government programs. But it's the church's job, not the government's, to meet the needs of the poor. The government often treats the needy impersonally, while the church has the potential to be sensitive to their dignity. We can also develop one-on-one relationships to meet their immediate physical needs—and then go on to focus on their longer-term physical and spiritual needs. Mother Teresa is one of the best examples in our time of serving the poor in a loving, compassionate way.

If you don't already know some needy people, please consider asking the Lord to bring one into your life. You can do so by praying this prayer: "Father God, by Your grace create in me the desire to share with the needy. Bring a poor person into my life so that I might learn what it really means to give." This will be a significant step in maturing your relationship with Christ.

May we echo Job's statement: *"I delivered the poor who cried for help, and the orphan who had no helper.... I made the widow's heart sing for joy.... I was eyes to the blind and feet to the lame. I was a father to the needy, and I investigated the case which I did not know"* (Job 29:12-16).

Secular charities

Numerous secular charities (schools, fraternal orders, organizations that fight diseases) compete vigorously for our donations. The Bible doesn't address whether we should give to these charities. Our family, however, has decided not to make these organizations part of our regular giving. Our reason is that even though many people support secular charities, only those who know the Lord support the ministries of Christ. We do, however, occasionally give to secular charities when the solicitor is a friend we want to encourage or influence for Christ, or we sense the Lord's specific prompting to give.

RECOMMENDED RESOURCES

The Treasure Principle by Randy Alcorn is an excellent book.

Generous Giving, **www.generousgiving.org**, has many proven resources to help you become more generous.

Brian Kluth, **www.kluth.org**, is an outstanding author and speaker.

For more recommended resources on generosity, log on to www.compass1.org and click on Resources.

LET'S GET PRACTICAL!

JOURNEY TO GENEROSITY

For most of us, becoming more generous is a journey that takes time. The more we expose ourselves to needs and what the Bible teaches about giving, the more generous we become. Follow these steps to make progress in your journey:

1. Describe where you are in your journey to generosity.

2. Complete the Generosity Grid.

Just as investors seek to grow investment portfolios on earth, so wise followers of Christ should view their giving as growing a giving portfolio in heaven. In Matthew 6:20, Jesus instructs us, *"Store up for yourselves treasures in heaven."* We believe that the Lord wants us to have an investor mentality when considering funding the work of God.

The grid on the next page is intended to help you evaluate your giving. Few will have a perfectly balanced giving portfolio. For most, their giving is going to be more heavily weighted toward a ministry or need for which God has given them a particular passion.

The top of the grid represents the basic categories of recipients: your church, evangelism, discipleship, and the needy. The other axis represents geography. Christ said, *"You shall be My witnesses both in Jerusalem, and in all Judea and Samaria, and even to the remotest part of the earth"* (Acts 1:8). Similarly, we have divided the geography into local (Jerusalem), national (Judea) and international (remotest parts of the earth).

Complete the grid using percentages or amounts of your giving.

	Church	Evangelism	Discipleship	Needy
Local				
National				
Global				
Total				

Do I view my giving as investing for eternity? If not, what can I do to develop this mind-set?

What am I most passionate about helping to fund? Why?

How can I be more effective in funding that for which God has given me a passion?

In light of the Giving Grid, do I need to be more generous with certain categories of recipients or geographies? If so, what will I do?

6

WORK

FACILITATORS GUIDE

"Whatever you do, do your work heartily, as for the Lord rather than for men . . .
It is the Lord Christ whom you serve" (Colossians 3:23-24).

WORK

Facilitators Guide for Week 6

Overview: Work can be fulfilling or frustrating. Our satisfaction depends on understanding the Lord's perspective of work.

Let's Get Practical!

☐ Complete the **Estimated Spending Plan (Budget)** on pages 150-156

☐ Complete the free **Personality Profile** by logging on to **www.compass1.org** and clicking on "Small Group Studies" and then "Personality Profile."

Agenda

1. __________ (5 minutes) Open in prayer.

2. __________ (5 minutes) Everyone individually recites from memory:

"Whatever you do, do your work heartily, as for the Lord rather than for men; knowing that from the Lord you will receive the reward of the inheritance. It is the Lord Christ whom you serve" (Colossians 3:23-24).

3.________ (85 minutes) Begin the group discussion.

Day One (Work)

Complete the Personality Profile by logging on to www.compass1.org, click on Small Group Studies Tools & Resources and then click on the Navigating Study Student and Facilitator Tools. **Also complete the Estimated Spending Plan** on pages 150-156.

1. Do you have any questions about your Personality Profile or Estimated Spending Plan?

2. What did you learn from completing them that will be helpful to you?

Read *Genesis 2:15.*

3. Why is it important to recognize that the Lord created work before sin entered the world?

[Work was initiated before sin entered the world. And in the perfect, sinless environment of the Garden of Eden, God created work for our benefit. It was not a result of sin and the curse.]

Read Genesis 3:17-19.

4. What was the consequence of sin on work and how have you experienced this in your work?

[Work became difficult because of sin.]

Read *Exodus 20:9* and *2 Thessalonians 3:10-12.*

5. What do these passages say to you about work and how are you applying them?

Exodus 20:9— [Old Testament believers were required to work six days a week.]

2 Thessalonians 3:10-12— [Work is also required in the New Testament. This verse does not recommend hunger for those who can't work because of physical or mental limitations—only those who are capable but choose not to work.]

Day Two (God's role in work)

Read *Genesis 39:2-5; Exodus 35:30-35* and *Psalm 75:6-7.*

1. What do these verses tell us about the Lord's involvement in our work, and how do these truths differ from the way most people view work?

Genesis 39:2-5— [The Lord controls success.]

Exodus 35:30-35— [The Lord gives us job skills and the ability to teach.]

Psalm 75:6-7— [The Lord controls promotion and demotion.]

2. How will this perspective influence your view of work?

Day Three (Employers & Employees)

Read *Ephesians 6:5-9; Colossians 3:22-25* and *1 Peter 2:18.*

1. What responsibilities do the employer and employee have, according to these verses?

Employee responsibilities: [Genuine obedience to employer; even one who is not good and gentle. Work hard as unto the Lord.]

Employer responsibilities: [An employer should serve and not threaten employees.]

2. For whom do you really work? How will this understanding change your work performance?

[We work for the Lord. This perspective will allow us to make a sincere effort—even in challenging situations—to serve those who are our superiors or our subordinates.]

* *Facilitator*, you should have approximately **one hour** of class time remaining.

Day Four (Working hard & resting)

Read *Proverbs 6:6-11; Proverbs 18:9* and *2 Thessalonians 3:7-9.*

1. What does the Lord say about working hard?

Proverbs 6:6-11— [Ants are honored for hard work, and those who are lazy are warned of poverty.]

Proverbs 18:9— [A lazy person is compared to someone who destroys.]

2 Thessalonians 3:7-9— [Paul modeled hard work.]

2. Do you work hard? If not, describe what steps you will take to improve your work habits.

Read Exodus 34:21.

3. What does this verse communicate to you about rest?

[Hard work should be balanced with adequate rest and other biblical priorities. Even during busy times, one day of rest a week was required.]

4. Do you get enough rest and how do you guard against overwork?

Day Five (Women working, partnerships & retirement)

Read *Proverbs 31:10-28* and *Titus 2:4-5*.

1. What do these passages tell us about women working?

Proverbs 31:10-28— [The excellent wife was diligent, worked with her hands, acquired and prepared food; invested, provided clothes for the family, and sold merchandise. She worked outside the home, but always with a focus toward the home.]

Titus 2:4-5— [Young wives were encouraged to be workers at home.]

2. If you are a woman, how does this apply to your situation?

Read *2 Corinthians 6:14-18.*

3. How does this concept of "yoking" or "being bound together" apply to partnerships in business and work?

[The principle of yoking applies to business partnerships. It is permissible for an employee to work for an employer who does not know Christ, but partnership with an unbeliever is discouraged.]

4. Can you give some examples from the Bible of people who retired?

[The Bible gives no examples of people retiring and provides only one direct reference to it, which is found in Numbers 8:24-26. This instruction applied only to the Levites who worked on the tabernacle.]

5. Do you think retirement, as it is practiced in our culture, is biblically acceptable? What are your retirement plans?

Day Six (the Notes)

Read the Work Notes on pages 138-149 and answer:

1. What in the notes proved especially helpful or challenging? How will you apply this to your work situation?

2. Do you usually realize you are working for the Lord? If not, what will you do to become more conscious of this?

I will take the following *action* as a result of this week's study:

Remaining Agenda

1. __________ (10 minutes) Play the Week 6 segment of the *Navigating Your Finances* DVD.
2. __________ (10 minutes) Note in the Prayer Logs requests and answers to prayers.
3. __________ (5 minutes) End in prayer.

WORK NOTES

Please read *after* completing Day 5 homework.

Over a lifetime, the average person spends about 100,000 hours working. But often with the job comes some degree of dissatisfaction. Perhaps no statistic demonstrates this more than job-change frequency. A survey found that the average man changes jobs every four and one-half years, and the average woman, every three years. Boredom, lack of fulfillment, inadequate wages, and countless other pressures contribute to this discontentment. Doctors, housewives, salespersons, blue-collar workers, managers, all—regardless of profession—have expressed similar frustrations. Understanding what God says about work will help you find satisfaction in your job. Implementing these principles will make you more valuable in the job market, and possibly position you to increase your income.

GOD'S PERSPECTIVE OF WORK

Despite what many believe, work was initiated for our benefit in the sinless environment of the garden of Eden. Work is not a result of the curse! *"The LORD God took the man and put him into the garden of Eden to cultivate it and keep it"* (Genesis 2:15). The very first thing the Lord did with Adam was put him to work.

After the fall, work became more difficult. *"Cursed is the ground because of you; in toil you will eat of it all the days of your life. Both thorns and thistles it shall grow for you; and you will eat the plants of the field; by the sweat of your face you will eat bread"* (Genesis 3:17-19).

Work is so important that in Exodus 34:21, God gives this command: *"You shall work six days."* The apostle Paul is just as direct: *"If anyone is not willing to work, then he is not to eat"* (2 Thessalonians 3:10). Examine the verse carefully. It says, *"If anyone is not willing to work."* It does not say, *"If anyone cannot work."* This principle does not apply to those who are physically or mentally unable to work; it is for those who are able but choose not to work.

A close friend of mine has a brother in his mid-forties whose parents have always supported him. He has never had to face the responsibilities and hardships involved in a job. Consequently, his character has not been properly developed, leaving him hopelessly immature in many areas of his life.

One of the primary purposes of work is to develop character. While the carpenter is building a house, the house is also building the carpenter. The carpenter's skill, diligence, manual dexterity, and judgment are refined. A job is not merely a task designed to earn money; it's also intended to produce godly character in the life of the worker.

ALL HONEST PROFESSIONS ARE HONORABLE

The Bible gives dignity to all types of work, not elevating any honest profession above another. David was a shepherd and a king. Luke was a doctor. Lydia was a retailer. Daniel was a government worker. Paul was a tentmaker. Mary was a homemaker. And, finally, the Lord Jesus Christ was a carpenter.

In God's economy, there is equal dignity in the labor of the janitor and the president of the company.

GOD'S PART IN WORK

Scripture reveals three responsibilities the Lord has in our work.

1. GOD GIVES JOB SKILLS.

Exodus 36:1 illustrates this truth: *"Every skillful person in whom the Lord has put skill and understanding to know how to perform all the work…shall perform."* God has given each of us unique aptitudes. People have a wide variety of abilities, manual skills, and intellectual capacities. It's not a matter of one person being better than another, merely that each has received different abilities.

2. GOD GIVES SUCCESS.

The life of Joseph is a perfect example of God helping a person to succeed. *"The Lord was with Joseph, so he became a successful man….His master saw that the Lord was with him and how the Lord caused all that he did to prosper"* (Genesis 39:2-3). Although we all have certain responsibilities, it is ultimately God who controls success.

3. GOD CONTROLS PROMOTIONS.

Psalm 75:6-7 says, *"For promotion and power come from nowhere on earth, but only from God"* (TLB). As much as it may surprise you, our bosses aren't the ones who control whether we will be promoted. Many people leave God out of work, believing that they alone are responsible for their abilities and success.

One of the major reasons they experience stress and frustration in their jobs is because they don't understand God's role in work.

Consider this question for a few minutes: If God gives you your abilities and controls success and promotion, how should this perspective affect your work?

OUR PART IN WORK

Did you know that in our work, we actually serve the Lord rather than people? Paul writes: *"Whatever you do, do your work heartily, as for the Lord rather than for men.... It is the Lord Christ whom you serve"* (Colossians 3:23-24).

Recognizing that we work for the Lord has profound implications. If you could see Jesus Christ as your boss, would you try to be more faithful in your job? The most important question you need to answer every day as you begin your work is this: "For whom do I work?" The Bible makes it clear: The person who signs your paycheck is *not* your ultimate employer. No matter where you are or what you do, you work for Christ Himself.

WORK HARD.

"Whatever your hand finds to do, do it with all your might" (Ecclesiastes 9:10, NIV). *"The precious possession of a man is diligence"* (Proverbs 12:27). Scripture encourages hard work and diligence, while laziness is strongly condemned: *"He who is slack in his work is brother to him who destroys"* (Proverbs 18:9).

Paul's life was an example of hard work. *"With labor and hardship we kept working night and day so that we might not be a burden to any of you...in order to offer ourselves as a model for you, so that you might follow our example"* (2 Thessalonians 3:8-9).

Your work should never be at such a level that people will equate laziness with God. Nothing less than hard work and the pursuit of doing the job well pleases Him. He doesn't require us to be "super-workers" who labor around the clock and never make mistakes, but He does expect us to pursue our responsibilities—whatever they may be—with diligence and integrity.

BUT DON'T OVERWORK!

Hard work, however, must be balanced by the other priorities of life. If your job demands so much of your time and energy that you neglect your relationship with Christ or your loved ones, then you're working too much. This applies to those in secular careers as well as those in full

-time Christian service. If you find that your relationship with Christ, your wife or husband, or your children is suffering, sit down with your spouse and ask yourself a direct question or two. Is the job itself too demanding, or is it more a matter of certain work habits that need adjustment? If you tend to be a workaholic, be careful not to shortchange the other priorities of life.

Exodus 34:21 reads, *"You shall work six days, but on the seventh day you shall rest; even during plowing time and harvest you shall rest."* We believe this Old Testament principle of resting one day out of seven has application today. This has been difficult for me, particularly during times of "plowing or harvesting," when a project deadline approaches or I'm under financial pressure.

When you think about it, rest can really become an issue of faith. Is the Lord *able* to make our six days of work more productive than seven? Of course He is! Our Creator instituted weekly rest for our physical, mental, and spiritual health. It's a day a week we can focus much of our time on getting to know the Lord even better. Philippians 3:8, 10 emphasizes the importance of this: *"I consider everything a loss compared to the surpassing greatness of knowing Christ Jesus my Lord...I want to know Christ and the power of his resurrection, becoming like him in his death."*

Study the following diagram to understand the balance God wants in our lives.

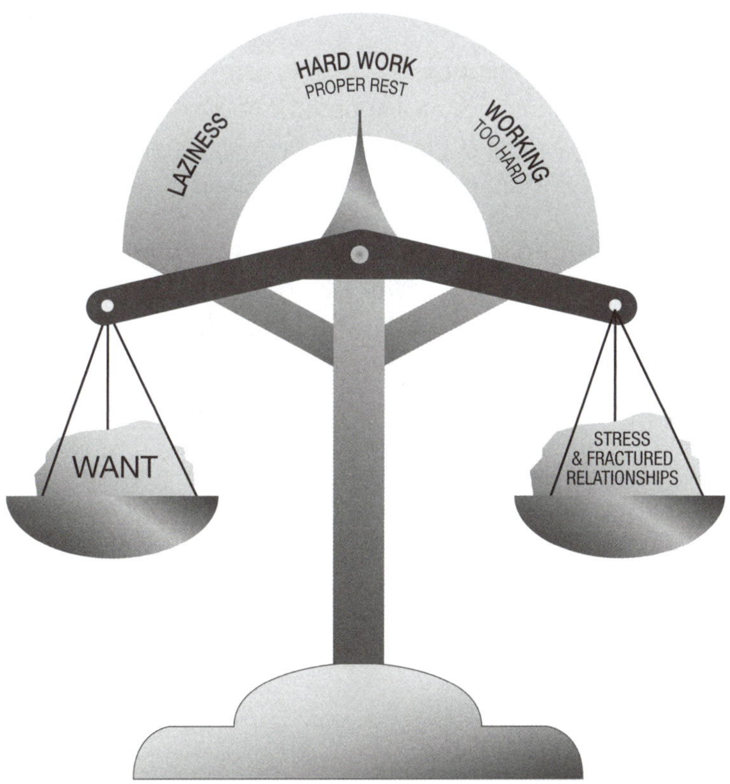

A balanced life with contentment

EMPLOYER'S RESPONSIBILITIES

Godly employers perform a balancing act. They are to love, serve, and encourage employees while leading them and holding them accountable for the completion of their assigned tasks. Let's examine several principles that should govern an employer's conduct.

1. SERVE YOUR EMPLOYEES.

The basis for biblical leadership is servanthood: *"Whoever wishes to become great among you shall be your servant"* (Matthew 20:26). Employers often concentrate on producing a profit at the expense of their personnel. The Bible, however, directs them to balance efforts to make a profit with an unselfish concern for employees, treating them with fairness and dignity. *"Masters* [employers], *grant to your slaves* [employees] *justice and fairness, knowing that you too have a Master in heaven"* (Colossians 4:1).

Employers should attempt to be creative as they serve their employees. For example, investing time and money to educate and upgrade their employees' job skills will help employees grow in value and earning power.

2. BE A GOOD COMMUNICATOR.

The Genesis account of building the tower of Babel supports the importance of good communication. At that time, everyone spoke the same language and adopted a common goal. The Lord makes this remarkable observation, *"If as one people speaking the same language they have begun to do this, then nothing they plan to do will be impossible for them"* (Genesis 11:6, NIV).

When people have good communication and pursue a common goal, then *"nothing they plan to do will be impossible for them"*—as long as it's within the will of God. Since building the tower was not what He wanted, He stopped construction. And how did God do it? He disrupted their ability to communicate, which was the foundation for successfully completing the tower. *"Come, let us go down and confuse their language so they will not understand each other"* (Genesis 11:7, NIV).

It is especially important to listen to employee complaints. *"If I have despised the claim of my…* [employees] *when they filed a complaint against me, what then could I do when God arises? And when He calls me to account, what will I answer Him?"* (Job 31:13-15). A sensitive, listening ear is a tangible expression of care. When a complaint is legitimate, employers should take appropriate steps to solve the problem.

3. HOLD EMPLOYEES ACCOUNTABLE.

Employers are responsible for employees knowing what's expected on the job. Employers should regularly evaluate employee performance, and communicate it to them. Employees who do not perform satisfactorily and who are unable or unwilling to change may require dismissal.

4. PAY EMPLOYEES A FAIR WAGE PROMPTLY.

The Bible warns employers to pay a fair wage. "[The Lord will judge] *those who oppress the wage earner in his wages"* (Malachi 3:5). It also commands them to pay wages promptly when due. *"You shall not oppress a hired* [employee].... *Give him his wages on his day before the sun sets...so that he will not cry against you to the LORD and it become sin"* (Deuteronomy 24:14-15).

5. PRAY FOR GODLY EMPLOYEES.

The Lord may choose to bless an employer for having a godly employee. Scripture gives two examples of this. First, *"Laban said to* [Jacob], *'If I have found favor in your eyes, please stay ...the LORD has blessed me because of you'"* (Genesis 30:27, NIV). Second, *"Joseph found favor in* [Potiphar's] *sight.... It came about that from the time he made* [Joseph] *overseer in his house and over all that he owned, the LORD blessed the Egyptian's house on account of Joseph; thus the LORD's blessing was upon all that he owned, in the house and in the field"* (Genesis 39:4-5).

This principle was my primary reason for employing Raymond, an especially godly construction worker. He was strong and did the work of two people, but far more important was his influence over the project. There was less profanity and pilferage, and he was an excellent model of hard work. This principle is not a command, but we believe wise employers will pray for the Lord to bring "Raymonds" to their companies.

EMPLOYEE'S RESPONSIBILITIES

We can identify six major responsibilities of godly employees by examining the story of Daniel in the lions' den. In the sixth chapter of Daniel, Darius, king of Babylon, appointed 120 people to administer the government, and three people—one of whom was Daniel—to supervise the administrators. Because of Daniel's outstanding service, the king decided to promote Daniel to govern the entire kingdom. Daniel's jealous peers looked for a way to disqualify him, but could find no basis for accusation. Knowing Daniel's devotion to God, they asked King Darius to enact a law requiring everyone to worship only the king, or die in the lions' den. Daniel refused to stop worshiping God, and Darius reluctantly threw him to the lions. When God rescued Daniel by sending an angel to shut the lions' mouths, the thankful king ordered all of his subjects to honor the God of Daniel. Daniel modeled the six characteristics of godly employees.

1. HONESTY

Daniel 6:4 tells us that Daniel's fellow employees could find no dishonesty in him, and there was no *"evidence of corruption"* in his work. To the chagrin of his enemies, Daniel was an example of total honesty, the crucial character quality we studied in Week 4.

2. FAITHFULNESS

We discover the second characteristic of godly employees in Daniel 6:4: *"He was faithful."* Godly employees strive for this. We want our employers to say, "I've always been able to depend on Heather because she's so faithful."

3. PRAYER

Godly employees are people of prayer. *"When Daniel knew that the document was signed* [restricting worship to the king alone]*... he continued kneeling on his knees three times a day, praying and giving thanks before his God, as he had been doing previously"* (Daniel 6:10). Daniel shouldered the responsibility of governing the most powerful country of his day. Few of us will ever face that kind of pressure or demands on our time. In spite of what must have been an extremely heavy schedule, however, Daniel knew and modeled the priority of prayer. If you aren't praying consistently, your work will suffer.

4. HONOR YOUR EMPLOYER

"Daniel spoke to the king, 'O king, live forever!'" (Daniel 6:21). What a remarkable response from Daniel. The king had been tricked into sentencing Daniel to the lions' den. But Daniel's reaction was to honor his employer—in spite of the terrible circumstance in which he found himself. Think how easy it would have been to disrespect the king and say something like, "You dummy! The God who sent His angel to shut the lions' mouths is now going to whack you!" Instead, he honored his employer in front of everyone.

Godly employees always honor their superiors. *"Servants* [employees], *be submissive to your masters* [employers] *with all respect, not only to those who are good and gentle, but also to those who are unreasonable"* (1 Peter 2:18). One way we honor employers is refusing to gossip behind their backs, regardless of their weaknesses.

5. HONOR FELLOW EMPLOYEES

People may damage your reputation or attempt to have you fired from your job to secure a promotion over you. Not only did they do that to Daniel, they even tried to murder him. Despite this, there is no evidence that he did anything but honor his fellow employees. *"Do not slander a servant* [employee] *to his master* [employer], *or he will curse you"* (Proverbs 30:10, NIV).

Godly employees avoid office politics and manipulation to secure a promotion. As we have already seen, your boss doesn't control your promotion; the Lord does. You can be content in your job as you focus on being faithful, honoring superiors, and encouraging other employees. Having done this, you can rest, knowing that Christ will promote you if and when He chooses.

6. VERBALIZE YOUR FAITH

King Darius would never have known about the Lord if Daniel hadn't communicated his faith at appropriate moments while at work. *"The king spoke and said to Daniel, 'Daniel, servant of the living God, has your God, whom you constantly serve, been able to deliver you from the lions?'"* (Daniel 6:20). Daniel's words and actions influenced King Darius, who observed his honesty, faithfulness, and hard work. Listen to the king's response: *"I issue a decree that in every part of my kingdom people must fear and reverence the God of Daniel. For He is the living God and He endures forever"* (Daniel 6:26, NIV).

Daniel influenced his employer, one of the most powerful people in the world, to believe in the only true God. You have that same opportunity in your God-given sphere of work.

Let me say this another way. A job well done earns you the right to tell others with whom you work about the reality of Christ. Viewing your work from God's perspective turns dissatisfaction to contentment with a job well done; drudgery becomes excitement over the prospect of introducing others to the Savior.

OTHER WORK ISSUES

RETIREMENT

The dictionary defines retirement as "withdrawal from an occupation, retreat from an active life." Our culture promotes the goal of retirement and ceasing all labor to pursue a life filled with leisure. Is this a biblical goal?

Numbers 8:24-26—the only reference to retirement in the Bible—applied specifically to the Levites working in the tabernacle. While people are physically and mentally capable, *there is no scriptural basis for retiring and becoming unproductive*—the concept of putting an older but able person "out to pasture." Don't let age stop you from finishing the work God has called you to accomplish. He will provide you with the necessary strength and mental clarity. Remember Moses! He was 80 years old when he began his 40-year adventure of leading the children of Israel.

The Bible does imply, however, that the type or intensity of work may change as we grow older—shifting gears to a less demanding pace to become more of an "elder seated at the gate." During this season of life, we can use the experience and wisdom gained over a lifetime. If we have sufficient income to meet our needs apart from our jobs, we may choose to leave work to invest more time in serving others as God directs.

AMBITION

Scripture doesn't condemn ambition. Paul was certainly ambitious, writing: *"We also have as our ambition…to be pleasing to Him"* (2 Corinthians 5:9). The Bible does, however, condemn *selfish* ambition. The Lord *"will render to each person according to his deeds…to those who are selfishly ambitious…wrath and indignation"* (Romans 2:6, 8). *"But if you have…selfish ambition in your heart, do not be arrogant and so lie against the truth. This wisdom is not that which comes down from above, but is earthly, natural, demonic. For where…selfish ambition exist, there is disorder and every evil thing"* (James 3:14-16). *"But you, are you seeking great things for yourself? Do not seek them"* (Jeremiah 45:5).

Remember, the Bible is not the enemy of ambition, only of the wrong type of ambition. Our ambition should be to please Christ, work hard, and be faithful in our job to please Him.

YOUR CALLING

God has given each of us a specific calling or purpose. *"We are His workmanship, created in Christ Jesus for good works, which God prepared beforehand so that we would walk in them"* (Ephesians 2:10). Study this passage carefully. *"We are His workmanship."* The Amplified Bible says, *"We are His handiwork."* God has given each of us special physical, emotional, and mental abilities. You may have heard the expression, "After the Lord made you, He threw away the mold." It's true! You are gifted uniquely. No one in all of history—past, present or future—is like you.

The passage continues, *"created in Christ Jesus for good works, which God prepared beforehand so that we would walk in them."* The Lord created each of us for a particular task, endowing us with the abilities and desires to accomplish it. Your calling may be full-time Christian service or a secular job.

People often wonder whether God wants them to continue in their work after they commit their lives to Christ. Many feel they may not be serving Him in a significant way if they remain at their jobs. Nothing could be further from the truth. The key is for each person to identify God's call for his or her life. Stanley Tam addresses this in his book, *God Owns My Business:* "Although I believe in the application of good principles in business, I place far more confidence in the conviction that I have a call from God. I am convinced that His purpose for me is in the business world. My business is my pulpit."

To those who earn a living through secular pursuits, it is a great comfort to know that the "call" of holy vocation carries over into all walks of life. The key is for us to identify God's call for our life, recognizing that God strategically places His children everywhere!

PARTNERSHIPS

Scripture discourages business partnerships with those who do not know Christ. In 2 Corinthians 6:14-17 we read, *"Do not be bound together with unbelievers; for what partnership have righteousness and lawlessness, or what fellowship has light with darkness?... or what has a believer in common with an unbeliever? …'Therefore, come out from their midst and be separate, says the Lord.'"*

Many have suffered financially—and in every other way—for violating this principle. We should also be careful about entering into any partnership, even with another Christian. With my lifetime of contacts, I would consider only a few people as partners. These are people I know well. I've observed their commitment to the Lord, know their strengths and weaknesses, and have seen them handle money faithfully.

If, after prayerful consideration, you decide to form a partnership, first take the time to commit your understandings into writing. Develop this agreement with your future partner, and be sure to include a way to end the partnership. If you aren't able to agree in writing, don't become partners. Remember, don't rush into any partnership without prayer and plenty of godly counsel.

PROCRASTINATION

A procrastinator is someone who, because of laziness or fear, has a habit of putting things off until later. This habit often develops into a serious character flaw.

The book of Ruth introduces Boaz, one of my favorite examples in the Bible of a non-procrastinator. Ruth's mother-in-law, Naomi, made this revealing comment about Ruth's future husband, Boaz: *"Wait, my daughter, until you know how the matter turns out; for the man will not rest* ***until he has settled it today"*** (Ruth 3:18, emphasis added). Boaz had a reputation for acting promptly.

Here are some practical suggestions to help overcome procrastination:

1. List the things you need to do each day.
2. Prayerfully review the list and prioritize it according to the tasks you need to accomplish first.
3. Finish the first task on your list before starting the second. Often that first task is the most difficult or the one you fear the most.
4. Ask the Lord to give you courage, remembering Philippians 4:13, *"I can do all things through Him who strengthens me."*

WIVES WORKING OUTSIDE THE HOME

For many reasons, women work in jobs of all kinds. Married women work to provide additional income for their families, to express their creativity, or because they simply enjoy their jobs. Single women work to provide their needs.

In our opinion, unless family finances prohibit it, it is wise during the children's early formative years for the mother to be home while the children are home. Titus 2:4-5 reads, *"Encourage the young women to love their husbands, to love their children, to be sensible, pure, workers at home."* As the children mature, a mother will have increased freedom to pursue outside work.

Proverbs 31:10-31 says, *"An excellent wife...does him* [her husband] *good and not evil all the days of her life. She looks for wool and flax and works with her hands. ...She brings her food from afar. She rises also while it is still night and gives food to her household.... She considers a field and buys it; from her earnings she plants a vineyard. ...She stretches out her hands to the distaff, and her hands grasp the spindle. She extends her hand to the poor.... She makes coverings for herself; her clothing is fine linen and purple. Her husband is known in the gates, when he sits among the elders of the land. She makes linen garments and sells them, and supplies belts to the tradesmen.... She looks well to the ways of her household, and does not eat the bread of idleness."*

Proverbs 31 paints a picture of the working wife living a balanced life, with the thrust of her activity toward the home. Some women are gifted as homemakers, and there is no more important task than raising godly children. Other women may have skills they desire to express in work outside the home, and some must work to earn income. Either way, it's a decision that the married couple should make together.

TWO-INCOME FAMILIES

If both the husband and wife work outside the home, it is worth examining how much income, after taxes and expenses, the second wage contributes. The "Example 1" column of the worksheet on the next page makes the following assumptions: 40 hours a week at $9 per hour; giving 10 percent of the gross income; federal income tax of 25 percent (a second income is added to the first and may be taxed at an even higher rate); state income tax of 5 percent; Social Security tax of 7.5 percent; ten trips per week of five miles at a cost of 25 cents a mile; lunch, snacks, and coffee breaks of $15 per week; eating out more often and using convenience foods add $35 a week to the budget; $20 for extra clothing and cleaning; $5 more for grooming; extra child care of $45 a week. The "Example 2" column assumes earning $25 an hour; all other assumptions remain the same.

These assumptions are for illustration only and may not represent your situation. Complete the exercise on the following page to determine your actual income after expenses.

Second Wage Earner Income and Spending

	Example 1	Example 2	Your Situation
Second wage earner gross yearly income:	$18,720.00	$52,000.00	____________
Second wage earner gross weekly income:	$ 360.00	$ 1,000.00	____________
Weekly Expenses:			
Giving	$ 36.00	$ 100.00	____________
Federal income tax	$ 90.00	$ 250.00	____________
State income tax	$ 18.00	$ 50.00	____________
Social Security tax	$ 27.00	$ 75.00	____________
Transportation	$ 15.00	$ 15.00	____________
Lunch/snacks/coffee breaks	$ 15.00	$ 15.00	____________
Restaurants/convenience food	$ 35.00	$ 35.00	____________
Extra clothing/cleaning	$ 20.00	$ 20.00	____________
Personal grooming	$ 5.00	$ 5.00	____________
Child care	$ 45.00	$ 45.00	____________
Total weekly expenses:	$ 306.00	$ 610.00	____________
Net additional family income:	$ 54.00	$ 390.00	____________
Net income per hour:	$ 1.35	$ 9.75	____________

Couples are often surprised to learn that the income earned by a second working spouse isn't as much as they had expected. Some have actually produced *more* net income (after reducing work-related expenses) when they decided to work in some creative way while staying at home. Of course, the financial benefits aren't the only factors to evaluate. Also consider the physical and emotional demands of working and how they affect a family.

LET'S GET PRACTICAL!

PERSONALITY PROFILE

As we learned in Ephesians 2:10, *"We are His workmanship, created in Christ Jesus for good works, which God prepared beforehand so that we would walk in them."* God has given each of us special physical and mental abilities and personalities.

It was eye-opening for me to discover some of the unique ways God made me—and it will be for you. Not recognizing how you were made can lead to frustration in your work, simply because you might be in a job for which you are not well-suited.

If you are married, not recognizing each other's personality can damage your relationship. It was a major breakthrough when Bev and I discovered ours. Why we acted and responded the way we did suddenly made sense, allowing us to respect each other's differences and reach a middle ground instead of constantly arguing. For the first time, we understood how to work together on our finances.

There is an excellent online assessment tool that has helped thousands understand how God made their personality. *It is completely free.* Log on to compass1.org, click on Small Group Studies Tools & Resources and then click on the Navigating Study Student and Facilitator Tools.

ESTIMATED SPENDING PLAN

Do you know how your great-grandparents kept a budget before people used checks, credit and debit cards and online banking? Simple! They used the cash-in-the-envelope system. They labeled envelopes for various spending categories and at the beginning of the month put a budgeted amount of cash in each envelope. And, for example, when the "clothes" envelope was empty, they didn't spend any more on clothes that month. It was simple and effective.

You'll use a similar system whether you use the Compass pencil and paper Spending Plan or the electronic spread sheet version.

You've been tracking your income and spending for 30 days, and you're now ready to complete your Estimated Spending Plan on pages 155-156 or download the electronic version from **www.compass1.org**.

For many, this can be challenging, because you may be discouraged to learn you're spending more than you're earning. *But take heart–there is hope.* Every week for the rest of the study you will be refining a workable Spending Plan.

Complete the following steps:

1. LIST YOUR INCOME.

List all your income in the "Income" section of the Estimated Spending Plan.

Many people don't receive steady, predictable income. This is especially common for the self-employed and commissioned salesperson. If your income is not consistent, estimate your yearly income and divide by 12 to determine your average monthly income.

Business expense reimbursements should not be considered income. Avoid the temptation to spend expense money as if it were income. This can lead to increased debt when those bills come due.

2. LIST YOUR EXPENSES.

Review your 30 Days of Tracking on pages 44-45. Then complete and total each expense category on the Estimated Spending Plan. We've designed it to be very detailed to help you identify what you are actually spending. After you complete and total the 12 expense categories, add them together to determine your total expenses.

Not all spending is consistent each month. Spending that varies includes:

- *Irregular monthly expenses* - such as food and utility bills. Simply estimate what you spend in an average month. As you continue to use the Spending Plan, you will become more accurate in projecting these expenses.
- *Expenses that don't occur every month* - such as auto maintenance, medical bills, clothing, and vacations. Use the list on the next page to compute the average monthly cost by estimating the annual amount spent for an item and dividing by 12. For example, if you spend $600 a year for home repairs, set aside $50 a month to pay for repairs.

Expense Item	Annual Amount		Monthly Amount
Home Insurance	______________	÷ 12 =	________________
Real Estate Taxes	______________	÷ 12 =	________________
Home Repairs	______________	÷ 12 =	________________
Medical Bills	______________	÷ 12 =	________________
Life Insurance	______________	÷ 12 =	________________
Health Insurance	______________	÷ 12 =	________________
Disability Insurance	______________	÷ 12 =	________________
Auto Insurance	______________	÷ 12 =	________________
Replace Car	______________	÷ 12 =	________________
Clothing	______________	÷ 12 =	________________
Tuition	______________	÷ 12 =	________________
Vacation	______________	÷ 12 =	________________
Other	______________	÷ 12 =	________________

3. DETERMINE YOUR SURPLUS OR DEFICIT.

At the bottom of the Estimated Spending Plan, subtract the Total Expenses from your Total Income to determine whether you have a surplus or deficit.

Total Income: ___________

Minus Total Expenses: ___________

Equals Surplus or Deficit: ___________

If income is greater than expenses, you have a surplus and need only to control spending to maximize the surplus. Using a spending plan will help you accomplish this. *If expenses are greater than income,* you have a deficit and a careful review will be necessary to bring the Spending Plan into balance. You will begin to work on this next week.

ESTIMATED SPENDING PLAN (BUDGET)

Income	
Monthly Salary	4,200
Interest Income	25
Dividends	15
Commissions/Bonuses/Tips	0
Retirement Income	0
Net Business Income	0
Cash Gifts	10
Child Support/Alimony	0
Total Income	4,250

1. Giving	
Local Church	350
Poor & Needy	25
Ministries	50
Total Giving	425

2. Taxes	
Federal	600
Medicare/Social Security	50
State & Local Taxes	50
Total Taxes	700

3. Saving & Investing	
Emergency Savings	100
Auto Replacement	0
401k/ 403b/Retire Plans	0
College Funds	50
Stocks/Bonds/Other	0
IRA	50
Total Saving & Investing	200

4. Housing	
Mortgage	720
Prepay Mortgage	0
Property Tax	100
Homeowners/Flood Insurance	40
Rent	0
Renters Insurance	0
Electricity	100
Lawn Care/Gardening	5
Water/Sanitation	20
Telephone/Mobile Phone	45
Gas	0
Maintenance/Pool	40
TV/Cable/Satellite/Internet	25
Pest Control/Termite Bond	5
HOA/Condo Dues	0
Total Housing	1,100

5. Food	
Groceries	200
Eating Out	50
Total Food	250

6. Transportation	
Auto Payments	165
Gas & Oil	65
Auto Insurance	40
Licenses & Taxes	5
Repairs/Maint/Tires	25
Tolls/Transit Fares/Parking	0
OnStar/Satellite Radio	0

SAMPLE

AAA/Auto Club	0
Total Transportation	300

7. Clothing

Adults	55
Children/Diapers	25
Laundry/Dry Cleaning	10
Total Clothing	90

8. Medical & Health

Doctor	35
Dentist	20
Prescriptions	0
Eye Care/Glasses	20
Health/Vision/Dental Insurance	30
Disability Insurance	0
Long-Term Care Insurance	0
Deductibles	20
HSA/Flexible Spending	0
Total Medical & Health	125

9. Education

Adult Education	100
Kids Tuition/Supplies	25
Tutoring/Lessons/Activities	0
Total Education	125

10. Personal

Allowances	50
Child Care/Babysitting	25
Life Insurance	35
Liability Insurance	25
Cleaning Supplies	15
Toiletries/Cosmetics	15
Hair Care	65
Vitamins/Supplements	15
Gifts (Birthdays)	20
Gifts (Christmas)	30
Gifts (Anniversary/Weddings)	10
Gifts (Graduation)	5
Postage	5
Alimony/Child Support	0
Pet Food & Supplies	0
Veterinarian	0
Vaccinations & Prescriptions	0
Boarding/Pet Sitting	0
Tax Preparation/Legal	25
Sports/Hobbies	60
Bank Charges/Fees	0
Credit Card Charges/Fees	35
Family Pictures	5
Subscriptions/Dues	10
Total Personal	450

11. Entertainment/Vacations

Activities	25
Vacations/Travel/Motel	25
Videos/Books/Music	50
Total Entertainment/Vacations	100

12. Debts 310

(See Debt List on pages 79-80)

Total Income:	4,250
Minus Total Expenses:	4,235
Equals Surplus or Deficit:	15

SAMPLE

ESTIMATED SPENDING PLAN (BUDGET)

Income

Monthly Salary ____________
Interest Income ____________
Dividends ____________
Commissions/Bonuses/Tips ____________
Retirement Income ____________
Net Business Income ____________
Cash Gifts ____________
Child Support/Alimony ____________
Total Income ____________

1. Giving

Local Church ____________
Poor & Needy ____________
Ministries ____________
Total Giving ____________

2. Taxes

Federal ____________
Medicare/Social Security ____________
State & Local Taxes ____________
Total Taxes ____________

3. Saving & Investing

Emergency Savings ____________
Auto Replacement ____________
401k/403b/Retire Plans ____________
College Funds ____________
Stocks/Bonds/Other ____________
IRA ____________
Total Saving & Investing ____________

4. Housing

Mortgage ____________
Prepay Mortgage ____________
Property Tax ____________
Homeowners/Flood Insurance ____________
Rent ____________
Renters Insurance ____________
Electricity ____________
Lawn Care/Gardening ____________
Water/Sanitation ____________
Telephone/Mobile Phone ____________
Gas ____________
Maintenance/Pool ____________
TV/Cable/Satellite/Internet ____________
Pest Control/Termite Bond ____________
HOA/Condo Dues ____________
Total Housing ____________

5. Food

Groceries ____________
Eating Out ____________
Total Food ____________

6. Transportation

Auto Payments ____________
Gas & Oil ____________
Auto Insurance ____________
Licenses & Taxes ____________
Repairs/Maint/Tires ____________
Tolls/Transit Fares/Parking ____________
OnStar/Satellite Radio ____________
AAA/Auto Club ____________
Total Transportation ____________

7. Clothing

Adults	______
Children/Diapers	______
Laundry/Dry Cleaning	______
Total Clothing	______

8. Medical & Health

Doctor	______
Dentist	______
Prescriptions	______
Eye Care/Glasses	______
Health/Vision/Dental Insurance	______
Disability Insurance	______
Long-Term Care Insurance	______
Deductibles	______
HSA/Flexible Spending	______
Total Medical & Health	______

9. Education

Adult Education	______
Kids Tuition/Supplies	______
Tutoring/Lessons/Activities	______
Total Education	______

10. Personal

Allowances	______
Child Care/Babysitting	______
Life Insurance	______
Liability Insurance	______
Cleaning Supplies	______
Toiletries/Cosmetics	______
Hair Care	______
Vitamins/Supplements	______
Gifts (Birthdays)	______
Gifts (Christmas)	______
Gifts (Anniversary/Weddings)	______
Gifts (Graduation)	______
Postage	______
Alimony/Child Support	______
Pet Food & Supplies	______
Veterinarian	______
Vaccinations & Prescription	______
Boarding/Pet Sitting	______
Tax Preparation/Legal	______
Sports/Hobbies	______
Bank Charges/Fees	______
Credit Card Charges/Fees	______
Family Pictures	______
Subscriptions/Dues	______
Total Personal	______

11. Entertainment/Vacations

Activities	______
Vacations/Travel/Motel	______
Videos/Books/Music	______
Total Entertainment/Vacations	______

12. Debts ______

(See Debt List on pages 79-80)

Total Income:	______
Minus Total Expenses:	______
Equals Surplus or Deficit:	______

7

SAVING & INVESTING

FACILITATORS GUIDE

"The wise man saves for the future, but the foolish man spends whatever he gets" (Proverbs 21:20, TLB)

"Steady plodding brings prosperity; hasty speculation brings poverty" (Proverbs 21:5, TLB).

SAVING & INVESTING

Facilitators Guide for Week 7

Overview

This week's objectives are to learn the biblical attitudes toward saving and investing, and to teach the scriptural framework for saving and investing. **The Facilitator should not recommend any specific investments or financial products or services. Compass—*finances God's way*™ assumes no liability for any actions taken related to specific investments or savings.**

Let's Get Practical!

☐ Complete **Your Net Worth Calculation** on page 179.

☐ Complete **Track & Tweak** your Compass budget on pages 179-182. Log on to www.compass1.org, click on Small Group Studies Tools & Resources and then click on the Navigating Study Student and Facilitator Tools.

☐ Check out **How to Increase Savings** on compass1.org, clicking on Small Group Studies Tools & Resources and then click on the Navigating Study Student and Facilitator Tools.

Agenda

1. _________(5 minutes) Open in prayer.

2. __________ (5 minutes) Everyone individually recites from memory:

"The wise man saves for the future, but the foolish man spends whatever he gets" (Proverbs 21:20, TLB).

"Steady plodding brings prosperity; hasty speculation brings poverty" (Proverbs 21:5, TLB).

3. __________(85 minutes) Begin the group discussion.

Day One (Saving)

Complete Your Net Worth Calculation and Track & Tweak Your Compass Spending Plan on pages 179-182. Then, log on to **www.compass1.org**, click on Resources and then click on the Navigating Study Student and Facilitator Tools to learn **How to Increase Savings.**

1. Do you have questions about any of these?

2. What did you learn from completing them that was helpful, and how will you apply it?

Read *Genesis 41:34-36; Proverbs 21:20* and *Proverbs 30:24-25.*

3. What do these passages say to you about savings?

Genesis 41:34-36— [Joseph saved during a time of plenty to prepare for a coming famine.]

Proverbs 21:20— [The wise save, but the foolish only spend.]

Proverbs 30:24-25— [Ants are commended as wise because they save.]

4. If you are not yet saving, how do you propose to begin?

Read *Luke 12:16-21, 34.*

5. Why did the Lord call the rich man a fool?

[The rich man was foolish because he stored up all his goods and was not rich toward God by giving generously.]

6. According to this parable, why do you think it is scripturally permissible to save only when you are also giving? How does this apply to you?

[If we only save and do not give, our hearts will be drawn away from Christ and to our possessions.]

Day Two (Saving goals)

Read *1 Timothy 5:8.*

1. What is a scripturally acceptable goal for saving?

[It's permissible to save to meet family needs.]

Read *1 Timothy 6:9.*

2. What is a scripturally unacceptable reason for saving?

[The desire to become rich is unacceptable. However, it's not wrong to become rich if it's a by-product of being a faithful steward.]

Read *1 Timothy 6:10.*

3. According to this verse, why is it wrong to want to get rich (refer to *1 Timothy 6:9)?* Do you have the desire to get rich?

[When we want to become rich, we are actually loving money. The desire to get rich is common and can destroy our fellowship with the Lord.]

Read *1 Timothy 6:11.*

4. What should you do if you have the desire to get rich?

[Flee from the desire and pursue godly living.]

Day Three (Investing)

Read *Proverbs 21:5; Proverbs 24:27; Proverbs 27:23-24; Ecclesiastes 3:1* and *Ecclesiastes 11:2.*

1. What investment principle(s) can you learn from each of these verses, and how will you apply them?

Proverbs 21:5— [Be a faithful, steady plodder and not hasty in investing.]

Proverbs 24:27— [Develop your means of producing an income before acquiring a house.]

Proverbs 27:23-24— [Know the status of your assets at all times.]

Ecclesiastes 3:1— [Timing is important when making investment decisions.]

Ecclesiastes 11:2— [Diversify your investments because you don't know what will happen.]

* *Facilitator,* you should have about **one hour** of class time remaining.

Day Four (Inheritance)

Read *Genesis 24:35-36; Proverbs 13:22* and *2 Corinthians 12:14.*

1. Should parents attempt to leave a material inheritance to their children? If so, how are you going to implement this principle?

[Yes, parents should attempt to leave an inheritance to their children.]

Read *Proverbs 20:21* and *Galatians 4:1-2.*

2. What caution should parents exercise?

Proverbs 20:21— [An inheritance should not be given into a child's care until the child is wise enough to manage it.]

Galatians 4:1-2— [The appointment of a guardian through a will or trust helps ensure a child's maturity before receiving an inheritance.]

Day Five (Gambling)

Gambling is defined as: playing games of chance for money, betting, and speculating. Some of today's most common forms of gambling are casino wagering, betting on sporting events, horse races, dog races and state-run lotteries.

1. What are some of the motivations that cause people to gamble, and do these motives please the Lord? Why?

[People are motivated to gamble by the desire to get rich quick, greed, and by the prospect of getting something for nothing. Many want to become wealthy so they can quit working. These motives do not please the Lord because they are contrary to His principles found in the Bible.]

Read *Proverbs 28:20* and *Proverbs 28:22*.

2. According to these passages, why do you think a godly person should not gamble?

[A person who hastens after wealth is identified as evil and will experience poverty. Please encourage your class never to bet one penny. State lotteries are particularly enticing because they have been legalized by the government and glamorized by the media.]

3. Are you committed never to gamble? Explain why or why not.

Day Six (the Notes)

Read the Saving & Investing Notes on pages 166-178.

1. What in the notes proved especially helpful?

2. Describe the specific steps you intend to take to begin saving and investing.

3. I will take the following *action* as a result of this week's study.

Remaining Agenda

1. __________ (10 minutes) Play the Week 7 segment of the *Navigating Your Finances* DVD.
2. __________ (10 minutes) Note in the Prayer Log requests and answers to prayers.
3. __________ (5 minutes) End in prayer.

Reminder

- Please recommend the participants who are qualified to be future facilitators.
- Encourage those who do not yet have a current will to secure one.
- Remind everyone to visit **www.compass1.org** and click on Resources for more practical information on investing.

SAVING & INVESTING NOTES

Please read after completing Day 5 homework.

The Bible contains very practical saving and investing advice. But before we take a look at what it says, we need to be aware of two important principles.

FINDING THE BALANCE

We need to balance our saving and investing with generosity. Jesus told a parable of a farmer who harvested a bumper crop and said to himself, "*'I have no place to store my crops.... I will tear down my barns and build bigger ones, and there I will store* ***all*** *my grain and goods....' But God said to him, 'You fool! ... This is how it will be with anyone who stores up things for himself but is not rich toward God.... For where your treasure is, there your heart will be also'*" (Luke 12:16-21, 34, emphasis added).

The key word in this parable is the word "*all*." Jesus called the farmer foolish because he saved everything, and didn't *balance* saving with giving. If we only pile up our investments, they will pull on our hearts like gravity. Our affection will be drawn away from God toward them because *"where your treasure is, there your heart will be also"* (Luke 12:34). However, if we give generously to God, we can invest *and* still love Him with all of our heart.

DANGER AHEAD

Let's face it—most people want to get rich. I'll never forget how surprised I was the first time I realized the Bible's caution against it: *"People who* ***want to get rich*** *fall into temptation and a trap and into many foolish and harmful desires that plunge men into ruin and destruction"* (1 Timothy 6:9, emphasis added). This verse declares that those who want to get rich give in to temptations and desires that ultimately lead to ruin. Wanting to get rich is incredibly dangerous, but why?

The next verse answers that question: *"For the love of money is a root of all kinds of evil. Some people, eager for money, have wandered away from the faith, and pierced themselves with many griefs"* (1

Timothy 6:10). When we want to get rich, we actually *love* money. That has consequences I witnessed firsthand. Mike, a close friend, became consumed by a desire to get rich. He finally abandoned his wife and four young sons, and later denied Christ.

For much of my life, I too wanted to become rich. Not just a little rich, but filthy rich! So dealing with this attitude in my own heart has been difficult. Here's what I discovered: When I wanted to get rich, my motivations were pride, greed, or an unhealthy urge to prepare for uncertain economic times. I loved *money.* However, after I learned God's perspective, my motive completely changed. I wanted to be a faithful steward, wisely investing the money God entrusted to me. I simply wanted to please Him. I loved *God.*

Is it wrong, then, to become rich? No, that's not what I'm saying here. Many heroes of the faith, such as Job, Abraham, and David, were rich. In fact, I rejoice when God enables a person who has been a faithful steward to prosper. *Nothing is wrong with becoming wealthy if it is a by-product of being faithful.*

OVERCOMING THE TEMPTATION

How then, can a believer in Christ overcome the love of money and the desire to become rich? Let me put it in two words: split and submit.

Paul told Timothy to *"flee from* [the desire to get rich], *you man of God, and pursue righteousness, godliness, faith, love, perseverance and gentleness"* (1 Timothy 6:11). When you become aware of a desire to get rich, run from it!

You might begin by analyzing just what it is that triggers your desire. I discovered a habit of dreaming about wealth when I would take a long car trip. I broke the habit by listening to Christian radio and music to help me concentrate on the Lord instead.

The ultimate way of escape is by submitting to the Lord. We can do this confidently because Jesus overcame a huge temptation to become rich. After fasting 40 days, He was tempted three times by the devil. Here's the final temptation: "[the devil] *led* [Jesus] *up and showed Him all the kingdoms of the world in a moment of time. And the devil said to Him, 'I will give You all this domain and its glory... if You worship before me'"* (Luke 4:5-7).

Jesus was offered all the kingdoms of the world in an instant. Because of His complete submission to God the Father, He was empowered by the same Holy Spirit who lives in us to resist that temptation.

I believe that our heavenly Father does not usually allow His children to prosper when they are motivated to get rich. Wanting to get rich—loving money—closely parallels greed. And *"greed...amounts to idolatry"* (Colossians 3:5). It is for our sake that the Father protects us from loving anything that would draw us away from Him.

SAVING

Unfortunately, most people are not consistent savers. Look at the graph below. It's shocking! Americans saved an average of 10.8 percent of their income in 1984. By 2006, their rate of saving had fallen to a *negative* one percent, the lowest savings rate in the past seventy-three years!

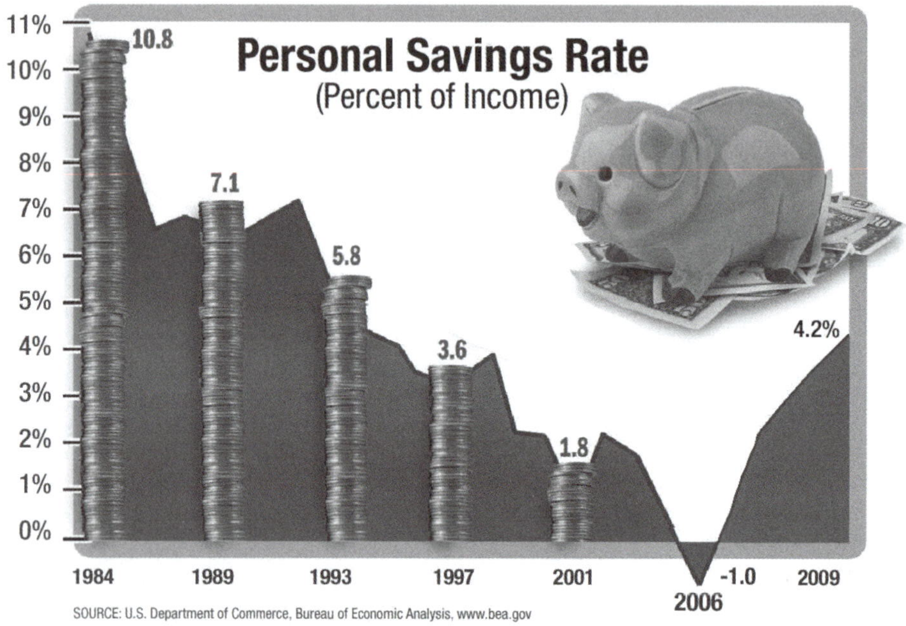

The Bible, on the other hand, encourages us to save: *"The wise man saves for the future, but the foolish man spends whatever he gets"* (Proverbs 21:20, TLB). God commends the ant for saving. *"Four things on earth are small, yet they are extremely wise: ants are creatures of little strength, yet they store up their food in the summer"* (Proverbs 30:24-25, NIV). We need to think like ants! Even though they are small, they save. You may not be in a position to save a lot right now, but begin the habit.

Joseph saved during *"seven years of great abundance"* (Genesis 41:29) in order to survive during *"seven years of famine"* (Genesis 41:30). That's what savings is all about: not spending today so that you'll have something to spend in the future. Most people are poor savers because they don't see the value in practicing self-denial. Our culture screams that we "deserve" to get what we want, when we want it!

The most effective way to save is to make it automatic. When you receive income, the first money you spend should be a gift to the Lord, and the second should go to savings. An automatic payroll deduction is a great way to save. Some people save their tax refunds or bonuses. Remember this: if you *immediately* save, you'll save more.

The Bible doesn't teach an amount to be saved. We recommend saving ten percent of your income. This may not be possible initially. But begin the habit of saving—even if it's only a dollar a month.

EMERGENCY SAVINGS

At Destination 1 on the Compass Map, you save $1,000 for emergencies—unexpected, unbudgeted expenses that whack us all.

Why save for emergencies? Because emergencies happen! The refrigerator goes on the fritz, the car brakes won't work, there's a health crisis in the family. And if you have saved the money for emergencies, you don't have to pile up more debt to pay for them. Then, you'll gradually increase emergency savings to three months' living expenses by Destination 3. Keep these savings in an account that is safe and easily accessible, such as a money market account with check-writing privileges.

INVESTING

***Compass—finances God's way*™ does not recommend any investments. No one is authorized to use affiliation with *Compass* to promote the sale of any investments or financial services.**

This chapter doesn't address everything you need to know about investing. Visit **www.compass1.org** for more helpful information. The Bible provides us with five basic guidelines for investing.

1. AVOID RISKY INVESTMENT.

God warns us to avoid risky investments, yet each year thousands of people lose money in highly speculative investments and scams. Ecclesiastes 5:13-15 says, *"There is another serious problem I have seen everywhere—savings are put into risky investments that turn sour, and soon there is nothing left to pass on to one's son. The man who speculates is soon back to where he began—with nothing"* (TLB).

How many times have you heard of people losing their life savings on some can't-miss-get-rich-quick scheme? Sadly, it seems that Christians are particularly vulnerable to scams because they trust others who appear to live by their same values. If you are offered an investment opportunity that seems too good to be true…it's probably too good to be true!

Avoid scams or risky investments by praying, seeking wise counsel, and doing your homework.

2. DIVERSIFY

Money can be lost on any investment. Stocks, bonds, real estate, gold—you name it—can perform well or poorly. Each investment has its own advantages and disadvantages. Since the perfect investment doesn't exist, we need to diversify and not put all our eggs in one basket. *"Divide your portion to seven, or even to eight, for you do not know what misfortune may occur on the earth"* (Ecclesiastes 11:2).

3. COUNT THE COST.

Every investment has costs: financial, time, effort, and sometimes even emotional stress. For example, a rental house will require time and effort to rent and maintain. If the tenant is irresponsible, you may have to try to collect rent from someone who doesn't want to pay—talk about emotions! Before you decide on any investment, consider all the costs.

4. THE LORD'S TIMING

The timing for the acquisition and sale of investments is especially important in this economic climate. Ecclesiastes 3:1 tells us: *"There is an appointed time for everything. And there is a time for every event under heaven."* The right investment at the wrong time is the wrong investment.

The decision to purchase or sell an investment is best made prayerfully. Despite what so-called financial experts and pundits so confidently express about what will happen to investments in the future, no one knows except the Lord. *No one*. Period!

God wants to be involved in every area of your finances, including investing. So humbly ask Him for wisdom as you consider an investment. Isaiah 48:17 says, *"I am the LORD your God, who teaches you what is best for you, who directs you in the way you should go."* In Luke 8:18, Jesus warns us, *"So take care how you listen."* You could paraphrase those words like this: *Be careful what you listen to.* And be especially careful of receiving investment advice from those who do not have a biblical view of money.

5. BE A STEADY PLODDER.

The fundamental principle for becoming a successful investor is to spend less than you earn, and regularly invest the surplus. In other words, be a steady plodder. The Bible says, *"Steady plodding brings prosperity, hasty speculation brings poverty"* (Proverbs 21:5, TLB). The original words for "steady plodding" picture a person filling a large barrel one handful at a time. Little by little the barrel is filled.

Nothing replaces consistent, month-after-month investing. Just do it—regardless of the investment climate—because when you do, your investments will grow through compounding.

Albert Einstein once said, "Compounding is the greatest mathematical discovery of all time, not $E=mc^2$." Compounding occurs when the earnings your investments produce are added to the principle, allowing *both* the earnings and the principle to grow exponentially.

UNDERSTANDING COMPOUNDING

There are three variables in compounding: the amount you save, the percentage rate you earn, and the length of time you save.

1. THE AMOUNT

The amount you save depends on your income and spending. We hope you will increase the amount available for saving as you learn God's way of handling money.

2. RATE OF RETURN

The second variable is the rate you earn on an investment. The following table demonstrates how an investment of $1,000 a year grows at various rates.

Rate Earned	Year 5	Year 10	Year 20	Year 30	Year 40
6%	5,975	13,972	38,993	83,802	164,048
8%	6,336	15,645	49,423	122,346	279,781
10%	6,716	17,531	63,003	180,943	486,851
12%	7,115	19,655	80,699	270,293	859,142

As you can see, an increase in rate has a remarkable effect on the amount accumulated. A two percent increase almost doubles the total over 40 years. But since higher returns usually also carry higher risks, be careful not to shoot for unrealistic returns.

3. TIME

Time is the third factor. Answer this: Who would accumulate more by age 65: Danielle, who started saving $1,000 a year at age 21, saved for eight years, and then completely stopped; or Matt, who saved $1,000 a year for 37 years starting at age 29? Both earned 10 percent. Is it Danielle, who saved a total of $8,000, or Matt, who saved $37,000? Check out the chart on the following page.

	Danielle		**Matt**	
Age	Contribution	Year-end Value	Contribution	Year-end Value
21	1,000	1,100	0	0
22	1,000	2,310	0	0
23	1,000	3,641	0	0
24	1,000	5,105	0	0
25	1,000	6,716	0	0
26	1,000	8,487	0	0
27	1,000	10,436	0	0
28	1,000	12,579	0	0
29	0	13,837	1,000	1,100
30	0	15,221	1,000	2,310
31	0	16,743	1,000	3,641
32	0	18,417	1,000	5,105
33	0	20,259	1,000	6,716
34	0	22,284	1,000	8,487
35	0	24,513	1,000	10,436
36	0	26,964	1,000	12,579
37	0	29,661	1,000	14,937
38	0	32,627	1,000	17,531
39	0	35,889	1,000	20,384
40	0	39,478	1,000	23,523
41	0	43,426	1,000	26,975
42	0	47,769	1,000	30,772
43	0	52,546	1,000	34,950
44	0	57,800	1,000	39,545
45	0	63,580	1,000	44,599
46	0	69,938	1,000	50,159
47	0	76,932	1,000	56,275
48	0	84,625	1,000	63,003
49	0	93,088	1,000	70,403
50	0	103,397	1,000	78,543
51	0	112,636	1,000	87,497
52	0	123,898	1,000	97,347
53	0	136,290	1,000	108,182
54	0	149,919	1,000	120,100
55	0	164,911	1,000	133,210
56	0	181,402	1,000	147,631
57	0	199,542	1,000	163,494
58	0	219,496	1,000	180,943
59	0	241,446	1,000	200,138
60	0	265,590	1,000	221,252
61	0	292,149	1,000	244,477
62	0	321,364	1,000	270,024
63	0	353,501	1,000	298,127
64	0	388,851	1,000	329,039
65	0	**427,736**	1,000	**363,043**

Incredibly, Danielle accumulated more because of the earlier start.

The following graph will help you visualize the benefits of compounding. If a person saves $2.74 a day—$1,000 a year—and earns 10 percent, at the end of forty years the savings will grow to $526,985 and will be earning $4,392 each month. However, if the person waits one year before starting, then saves for 39 years, the result won't be just $1,000 less; it will be $50,899 less! Compounding is your friend, and the earlier you can start it working for you, the better. Start saving and investing today!

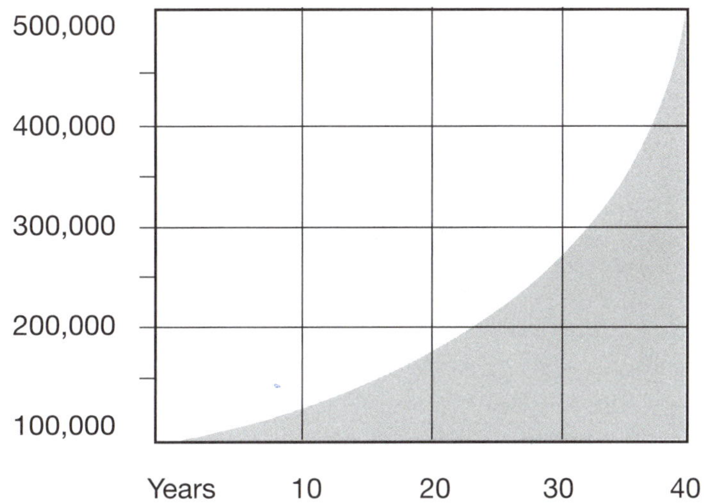

$1,000 Invested each year earning 10%

WHEN AND WHERE TO INVEST

Now, let's apply the investing principles found in the Bible.

We recommend three steps for investing. The strategy is to start conservatively and raise the percentage of higher-risk, higher-reward investments as the amount grows. Always maintain a foundation of conservative assets as a stable base upon which to build. If you are a savvy investor or have expertise in an area of investing, you will need to factor that in your personal strategy.

STEP 1 — 3 MONTHS SALARY INVESTED

Start your investment journey by investing in what are known as cash equivalents: *money market funds, certificates of deposit (CDs),* and *Treasury notes.*

Money market funds can be purchased through brokerage firms and banks. *CDs,* issued by banks, typically mature in lengths from three months to five years. If the bank issuing the CD is federally (FDIC) insured, your money currently is insured up to $250,000. *Treasury notes* are backed by the federal government and are free from state taxes. They mature in three months or longer.

Until you accumulate an amount equal to 3 months of your salary, your investment portfolio would look like this:

STEP 1

All Cash Equivalents

STEP 2 — 1 YEAR SALARY INVESTED

Once you have accumulated investments equal to 3 months of your salary, you are ready to begin Step 2, where you will increase your investments equal to 1 year of your salary.

We recommend you maintain a base of cash-equivalents, add conservative investments and some that are higher-risk, higher-reward. At Step 2, we suggest this mix for your investment portfolio:

STEP 2

25 percent: Cash-equivalents

50 percent: Balanced mutual fund, conservative stocks & bonds

25 percent: Higher-risk mutual funds and stocks and bonds

Definitions: Here are some basic investment definitions:

Mutual funds. The biggest advantage of investing in mutual funds is that you can apply the biblical principles of diversification and professional investment advice. There are many kinds of mutual funds. Some are composed of stocks, some of bonds; some contain both. Other mutual funds consist of international stocks or are limited in their selection to an investment, such as real estate. There are also many types of bond funds—those invested in government bonds, corporate bonds or tax-free municipal bonds. A *balanced mutual fund* invests in cash-equivalents, stocks and bonds. Choose funds that have solid track records for a minimum of ten years.

Stocks. When you buy a stock, you are purchasing part of a company. Generally, stocks have one of the greatest opportunities for profit, but you also can lose a lot if the company doesn't perform well. Some stocks pay a dividend.

Bonds. When you buy a bond, you *loan* money to a business or the government, and they pay you interest. Investors traditionally buy government bonds for safety, municipal bonds for tax-free returns, and corporate bonds for higher yields. It is important to realize that when interest rates rise, the value of bonds decline, and vice versa.

Real estate. People buy property for income or appreciation. There are tax advantages for owning buildings because depreciation is deductible. However, unlike publicly traded stocks or bonds that can be sold quickly, real estate may require a long time to sell.

It's usually smart to keep 25 percent of investments in cash-equivalents because it gives you flexibility and stability.

STEP 3 — MORE THAN 1 YEAR SALARY INVESTED

At Step 3, you have accumulated an amount equal to more than 1 year salary. We recommend the following mix of investments:

STEP 3

25 percent: Cash-equivalent

25 percent: Balanced mutual fund and conservative stocks and bonds

25 percent: Higher-risk, higher-return mutual funds and stocks and bonds

25 percent: Real estate & other investments

Remember, the name of the game is to be a faithful *steady plodder*—consistently adding to your investments and allowing them to compound.

Goals and time frame

When deciding where to invest, you need to consider your goals and time frame. This means using different investments for different goals. An investment that is suitable for a fifteen-year goal is simply not appropriate for money you will need in two years. If you need the down payment to buy your home in two years as opposed to funding your retirement in fifteen years, you will invest the money differently. Move your money into more conservative investments that can be more quickly converted into cash as you get closer to the time you will need to spend it.

Changing investment climate

The massive financial crisis of 2008-2009 has challenged many assumptions considered prudent for investing for decades, such as:

- Houses will always go up in value
- Buy a quality stock, and hold it forever, no matter what
- The dollar and government debt is rock solid

On the heels of governments around the world pouring trillions of borrowed or printed dollars into their economies to prevent the financial crisis from becoming a depression—there are issues you need to factor into your investment decisions. Will our country experience inflation or deflation? What will happen to the employment picture, and how will this impact you?

The good news is that God's investment principles work in any culture and in any economy.

GOD'S INSTRUCTIONS TO SUCCESSFUL INVESTORS

God realizes that when our assets increase, they can become a potential barrier to a close relationship with Him. If you have a lot of resources, the Lord isn't disappointed or surprised; rather, He entrusted them to you for a purpose.

In 1 Timothy 6:17-19, the Lord gives us instructions to help those with resources remain undistracted from loving and serving Him.

1. DON'T BE CONCEITED.

"Instruct those who are rich [successful investors] *in this present world not to be conceited"* (1Timothy 6:17). Wealth tends to produce pride. For several years, we drove two vehicles. The first was an old pickup truck that cost $100—and looked it! When I drove that truck to the bank drive-in window to cash a check, I was humble. I knew the cashier was going to carefully check my account to confirm that the driver of that beat-up truck had sufficient funds in his account. And when I received the money, I drove away with a song in my heart and praises on my lips.

Our other vehicle was a well-preserved, second-hand car that was expensive when it was new. When I drove that car to the bank, I appeared to be a different person. I was a person who deserved a certain amount of respect. I wasn't quite as patient when the cashier examined my account, and when I received the money, I wasn't as grateful. Wealth often leads to pride.

2. PUT NO CONFIDENCE IN YOUR ASSETS.

"Instruct those who are rich [successful investors] *in this present world not…to fix their hope on the uncertainty of riches, but on God, who richly supplies us with all things to enjoy"* (1 Timothy 6:17).

The ability to accumulate assets without placing our confidence in them is a massive struggle. Someone once observed, "For every ninety-nine who can be poor and remain close to Christ, only one can become affluent and maintain close fellowship with Him." It must be human nature to cling to the Lord when it's obvious that He must provide our needs. Once people reach financial freedom, however, they often take the Lord for granted because they no longer think they have as much need of Him.

When you have resources, the tendency is to first look to your money to solve problems, instead of first praying and seeking the Lord. We tend to trust in what we can see with our eyes, rather than in the invisible living God. King Solomon said it this way, *"The wealth of the rich is their fortified city; they imagine it an unscalable wall"* (Proverbs 18:11). We need to remind ourselves that wealth—like health—is completely uncertain, and can be lost in a heartbeat. The Lord alone can be fully trusted.

3. GIVE GENEROUSLY.

"Instruct them to do good, to be rich in good works, to be generous and ready to share, storing up for themselves the treasure of a good foundation for the future, so that they may take hold of that which is life indeed" (1 Timothy 6:18-19). The Lord wants successful investors to be generous, and tells them of two benefits: (1) real eternal treasures that they will enjoy forever, and (2) the blessing of *"taking hold of that which is life indeed."* By exercising generosity, they can live the fulfilling life God intends for them now.

OTHER ISSUES

GAMBLING AND LOTTERIES

Lotteries and gambling of all types are sweeping our country. Internet gambling is exploding. Each year one in four Americans gambles at a casino. The average church member gives $20 a year to international missions, while the average person gambles $1,174 annually.

Sadly, more than 6 million Americans (including 1.1 million teens) are addicted to gambling, with consequences that break the hearts of their loved ones. Although the Bible doesn't specifically prohibit gambling, its *get-rich-quick* motivation violates the steady plodding principle.

In my opinion, we should *never* participate in gambling or lotteries—even for entertainment. We shouldn't expose ourselves to the risk of becoming compulsive gamblers, nor should we support an industry that enslaves so many.

INHERITANCE

Parents should try to leave an inheritance. *"A good man leaves an inheritance to his children's children"* (Proverbs 13:22). But inheritances should not be disbursed until heirs have been trained to be wise stewards. *"An inheritance gained hurriedly at the beginning will not be blessed in the end"* (Proverbs 20:21). Consider sprinkling distributions over several years as heirs mature enough to handle the responsibility of money. Select trustworthy people to help supervise the finances of young heirs until they are capable stewards. *"As long as the heir is a child, he does not differ at all from a slave although he is owner of everything, but he is under guardians and managers until the date set by the father"* (Galatians 4:1-2).

WILLS

It's important to prepare financially for your death. As Isaiah told Hezekiah, *"Thus says the Lord, 'Set your house in order, for you shall die'"* (2 Kings 20:1). One of the greatest gifts you can leave your loved ones for that emotional time is an organized estate and a properly prepared will or revocable living trust. If you don't have a current will or trust, make an appointment this week with an attorney to prepare one.

LET'S GET PRACTICAL!
YOUR NET WORTH CALCULATION

Your net worth is easy to determine. Simply subtract your total debts on page 80 from your total assets on page 36.

Total Assets $______________

Minus Total Debts $______________

Equals Net Worth $______________

As you reduce your debts and increase savings and investments, your net worth will increase.

We recommend that you update your Personal Financial Statement (your list of assets and debts and your net worth) around the first of every year to gauge your financial progress. To download a copy of the Personal Financial Statement in the **Electronic Practical Application Spreadsheet**, log on to www.compass1.org, click on Small Group Studies Tools & Resources and then click on the Navigating Study Student and Facilitator Tools.

TRACK & TWEAK YOUR SPENDING PLAN

TWEAK YOUR SPENDING PLAN

Last week when you completed your Estimated Spending Plan and subtracted your spending from your income, did you have more income than spending? For many people the answer is no! They discover there is too much month at the end of the money. Your tasks this week are to tweak (balance) your Spending Plan and track your income and spending.

The first step is to check out the percentages.

CHECK OUT THE PERCENTAGES!

How much of your income should be spent on food, clothes, housing, and so forth? It's helpful to compare the percent of income you're spending for these items to recommended percentages that work for thousands of people. But remember, they are only *recommended.*

If you have unusually high or low income, these numbers could change dramatically. For example, if your income is very high, the percentage you spend on food will be much lower than a person who earns a fraction of your income.

If you are spending more than the recommended amount for an item, it may be necessary to reduce your spending in that area to enjoy a balanced Spending Plan.

PERCENTAGES

Item	~~**Actual %**~~	**Recommended %**
Giving	10%	10 – 15%
Saving	7%	5 – 15%
Housing	33%	30 – 40%
Food	10%	5 – 15%
Transportation	7%	10 – 15%
Clothing	3%	2 – 7%
Medical/Health	9%	5 – 10%
Education/Child Care	4%	2 – 7%
Personal	7%	5 – 10%
Entertainment/Vacation	2%	5 – 10%
Debts	8%	5 – 10%

SAMPLE

YOUR PERCENTAGES

Item	Actual %	Recommended %
Giving	_______	10 – 15%
Saving	_______	5 – 15%
Housing	_______	30 – 40%
Food	_______	5 – 15%
Transportation	_______	10 – 15%
Clothing	_______	2 – 7%
Medical/Health	_______	5 – 10%
Education/Child Care	_______	2 – 7%
Personal	_______	5 – 10%
Entertainment/Vacation	_______	5 – 10%
Debts	_______	5 – 10%

As you continue to track your income and spending on pages 186-187, you'll discover that your Spending Plan is always changing and in need of tweaking. Your income may change, the interest you earn will fluctuate, and spending certainly will not be static. You will constantly refine the Spending Plan with one simple objective in mind: *spend less than you earn!*

Using a Tweak Sheet each month will remind you to try to continue to reduce spending and increase income so that your monthly surplus will grow.

TWEAK SHEET

What to Tweak	Spending Reduced	Income Increased
Secured part-time job		$250
Eating out less	$120	
Cut the lawn	$ 60	
Brown bag lunch	$ 80	
Sell car with loan	$240	

SAMPLE

TWEAK SHEET

What to Tweak	Spending Reduced	Income Increased
______________________	__________	__________
______________________	__________	__________
______________________	__________	__________
______________________	__________	__________
______________________	__________	__________
______________________	__________	__________
______________________	__________	__________
______________________	__________	__________

TRACK YOUR SPENDING PLAN

As we mentioned last week, it's helpful to think of your Spending Plan as the old cash-in-the-envelope system. Envelopes were labeled for various spending categories and at the beginning of the month a budgeted amount of cash was deposited in each envelope. It was simple and effective. When an envelope was empty, you stopped spending!

Think of each of the 12 spending categories as an envelope. Instead of depositing cash, you will use an "Estimated Amount" for the month to spend. And instead of taking cash out of an envelope, you just record what you spend. It's easy to always know exactly how much you have left to spend.

You will track income and spending, using the form on pages 186-187. Here's how to use it.

1. Fill in the monthly "Estimated Amount." From your Estimated Spending Plan on pages 155-156, fill in the Estimated Amount for each category. For example, giving is $425.

2. Record your income and spending for the month. And if you are using the paper Spending Plan, don't forget to use a pencil to make changes easily.

Anytime you can easily find out how you're doing simply by adding all you have spent for a category and comparing it to your Estimated Amount. We suggest you do this for every category midway through the month on the line titled "This Month Subtotal" to help you monitor your progress.

3. At the end of the month, total each category on the "This Month Total" line. Subtract this from the "Estimated Amount" to determine "This Month Surplus/(Deficit)."

4. How you are doing Year To Date?

To determine how well you are doing in each category for the year:

- Add this month's "Estimated Amount" to the previous month's "Year-to-Date Estimated Am't" to calculate the current "Year-to-Date Estimated Am't."
- Then add "This Month Total" to last month's "Year-to-Date Actual" to find the current "Year-to-Date Actual."
- Subtract the "Year-to-Date Actual" from the "Year-to-Date Estimate" to determine whether you have a surplus or deficit.

If you are not a math whiz, the description of the mathematical part of the Spending Plan can be confusing until you've done it for a few months. If you are using the Compass electronic Spending Plan, all these calculations will be automatically done for you!

SPENDING PLAN BIG PICTURE

Tracking Totals

This Month			Previous Month YTD			Year to Date	
Total Income	$4,375	+	Total Income	$33,725	=	Total Income	$38,100
minus Total Expenses	$4,210		minus Total Expenses	$35,142		minus Total Expenses	$39,352
= Surplus/(Deficit)	$ 165		= Surplus/(Deficit)	$(1,417)		= Surplus/(Deficit)	$(1,252)

This Month

Check out the three boxes at the bottom of the Spending Plan to discover the big picture of how you are doing. In the box titled "This Month," enter "This Month Total" income and "This Month Total" expenses, and subtract the expenses from the income to determine the surplus or the deficit for the month.

Year to Date

To discover how you're doing for the year, in the "Previous Month YTD" box enter the figures from last month's "Year to Date" box. Then add the figures from the "This Month" box to the "Previous Month YTD" box to arrive at the totals for the "Year to Date" box.

Congratulations! You've now started using your Spending Plan! It's a journey that becomes easier as you do it, so don't give up. The benefits of getting out of debt, giving and saving more, and enjoying financial health are worth the effort.

TRACKING SPENDING PLAN

Month: September **Year:** 2011

Category	INCOME	GIVING	TAXES	SAVE/INVEST	HOUSING	FOOD
Estimated Amount	$4,250	$425	$700	$200	$1,100	$250
Date						
1	2,100		350	100	860	
2						
3		100				80
4						
5						
6						
7						90
8						
9						
10	25	100			43	
11						
12						
13						
14						32
15						
Subtotal	2,125	200	350	100	903	202
16	2,100		350	100		
17		100				
18						41
19	50					
20					7	
21						
22						19
23	25					
24		100				
25						
26					56	
27	75					
28						
29					4	
30						50
31						
This Month Total	4,375	400	700	200	970	312
This Month Surplus/(Deficit)	125	25	0	0	130	(62)
YTD Estimated Am't	38,250	3,825	6,300	1,800	9,900	2,250
Year-to-Date Actual	38,100	3,900	6,300	1,800	10,350	2,000
Surplus/(Deficit)	(150)	(75)	0	0	(450)	250

Tracking Summary

This Month			**Previous Month YTD**			**Year to Date**	
Total Income	$4,375	=	Total Income	$33,725	+	Total Income	$38,100
minus Total Expenses	$4,210		minus Total Expenses	$35,142		minus Total Expenses	$39,352
= Surplus or (Deficit)	$ 165		= Surplus or (Deficit)	$(1,417)		= Surplus or (Deficit)	$(1,252)

SAMPLE

TRANSP.	CLOTHING	MED/HEALTH	EDUCATION	PERSONAL	ENTER/ VAC	DEBT
$300	$90	$125	$200	$450	$100	$310
		65		21		
			30		12	
15						
	20			35		
			190		40	120
				76		
215	15					
				9		
						25
		11				
				50		
230	35	76	220	191	52	145
				20		
15						
	42	5			7	20
				17		
				82		
15						
					40	
				23		
			11			
	16			110	46	80
15		65				
						50
275	93	146	231	443	145	295
25	(3)	(21)	(31)	7	(45)	15
2700	810	1125	1800	4050	900	2655
3120	670	1240	1780	4650	887	2655
(420)	140	(115)	20	(600)	13	0

SAMPLE

TRACKING SPENDING PLAN

Month: ______________________ **Year:** ________

Category	INCOME	GIVING	TAXES	SAVE/INVEST	HOUSING	FOOD
Estimated Amount						
Date						
1						
2						
3						
4						
5						
6						
7						
8						
9						
10						
11						
12						
13						
14						
15						
Subtotal						
16						
17						
18						
19						
20						
21						
22						
23						
24						
25						
26						
27						
28						
29						
30						
31						
This Month Total						
This Month Surplus/(Deficit)						
YTD Estimated Am't						
Year-to-Date Actual						
Surplus/(Deficit)						

Tracking Summary

This Month			Previous Month YTD			Year to Date	
Total Income	$________		Total Income	$________		Total Income	$________
minus Total Expenses	$________	=	minus Total Expenses	$________	+	minus Total Expenses	$________
= Surplus/(Deficit)	$________		= Surplus/(Deficit)	$________		= Surplus/(Deficit)	$________

TRANSP.	CLOTHING	MED/HEALTH	EDUCATION	PERSONAL	ENTER/ VAC	DEBT

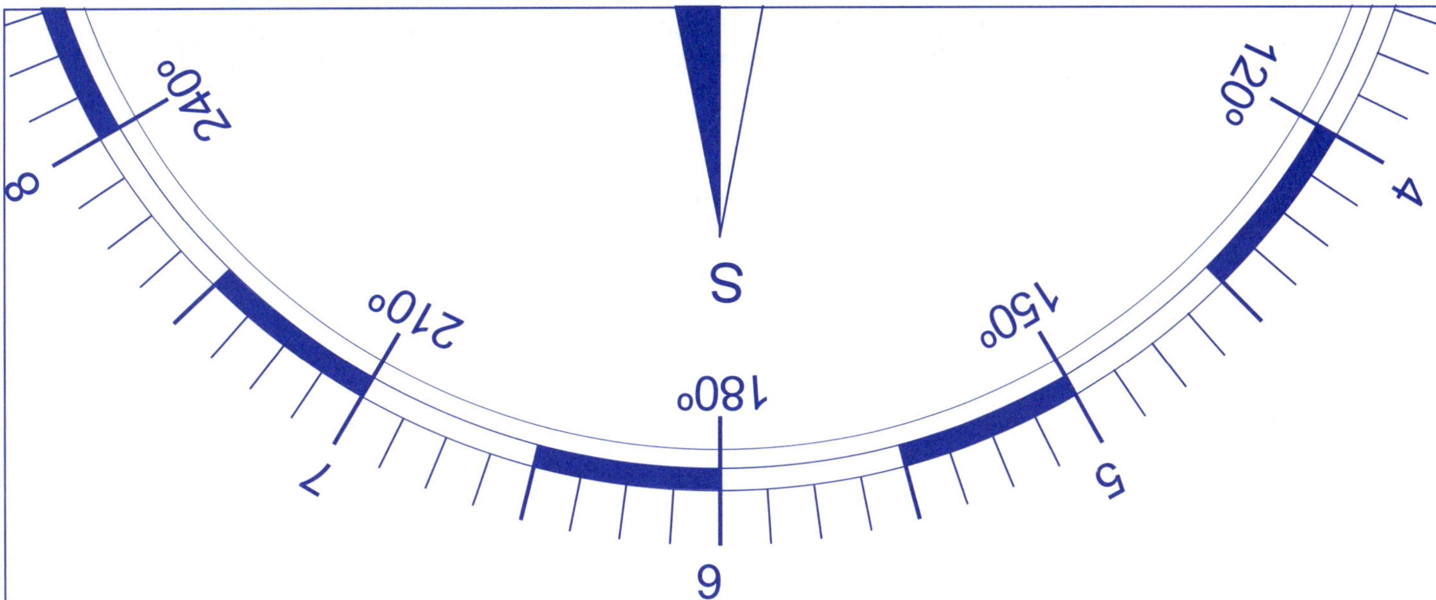

8

CRISIS & PERSPECTIVE

FACILITATORS GUIDE

*"For I have learned to be content in whatever circumstances I am.
I know how to get along with humble means, and I also know how to live
in prosperity… I can do all things through Him
who strengthens me"* (Philippians 4:11-13).

CRISIS & PERSPECTIVE

Facilitators Guide for Week 8

Let's Get Practical!

☐ Complete **Organizing Your Estate** on pages 223-228.

☐ Complete the **Crisis Budget** on pages 229-230.

☐ Secure a current will if you do not yet have one.

Agenda

1.__________ (5 minutes) Open in prayer.

2.__________ (5 minutes) Everyone individually recites from memory:

"For I have learned to be content in whatever circumstances I am. I know how to get along with humble means, and I also know how to live in prosperity… I can do all things through Him who strengthens me" (Philippians 4:11-13).

3.__________ (85 minutes) Begin the group discussion.

Day One (Crisis)

Complete Organizing Your Estate and the Crisis Budget on pages 223-230.

1. Do you have any questions about **Organizing Your Estate** and the **Crisis Budget**?

2. What did you learn from completing them that was helpful, and how will you apply what you learned?

Read *Romans 8:35, 37; Daniel 4:34-35* and *Jeremiah 32:17.*

3. Why do you think it is important to realize that God loves you and is in control of the situation when you are facing a crisis?

[A crisis can be frightening and discouraging. So, it's crucial to recognize that the Lord loves and cares deeply for you. He is powerful and ultimately controls all the difficult events.]

Day Two (Our response during a crisis)

Read *Romans 8:28-29.*

1. According to this passage, what does the Lord want to accomplish in our lives when we experience difficulties?

[God's objective during a crisis is to use it to conform us to Christ.]

2. Share a crisis you've experienced and how God used it to help you grow closer to Christ.

Read *James 1:2-4 and 1 Thessalonians 5:18.*

3. According to these verses, what should our attitude be in the midst of a crisis?

James 1:2-4— [We are to consider difficulties joyfully because they will help us mature in our relationship with Christ.]

1 Thessalonians 5:18— [We are to give thanks in all circumstances because the difficulties are God's will and intended for our benefit.]

4. How do you maintain this attitude when facing difficulties?

Day Three (Crisis preparation & Prosperity)

Read *Matthew 7:24-25.*

1. What should you do to prepare financially for future challenges and crises? On a scale of 1 to 10 (with 10 being the best), how well are you prepared?

[We are to learn and apply God's financial principles so that when the storms of life strike, we will have built our finances on the rock-solid truth of God's word.]

2. If you are not well-prepared, what will you do?

Read *Deuteronomy 30:15-16; Joshua 1:8* and *Hebrews 11:36-40.*

3. What do these passages say to you about financial prosperity for the believer?

Deuteronomy 30:15-16— [One of the blessings of obedience was prosperity.]

Joshua 1:8— [Knowing and obeying all God's commands resulted in prosperity.]

Hebrews 11:36-40— [Even godly people experience poverty and difficulties while exercising faith.]

Read *Genesis 37:23-28; Genesis 41:12-41; 2 Corinthians 11:23-27* and *Philippians 4:11-12.*

4. Did these godly people experience periods of financial abundance and at other times a lack of it?

[Yes, they experienced times of abundance and times of want.]

5. Was their lack a result of sin and a lack of faith? And do you think all Christians should always prosper financially? Why?

[Joseph's and Paul's poverty was not because of a lack of faith or sin. Once a person has been a faithful steward in every area, he or she is in a position for the Lord to prosper. However, God may not because (1) He is building our character (Romans 5:3-4); or (2) He disciplines us in order to encourage us to forsake sin (Hebrews 12:6, 10); or (3) God's sovereignty (Hebrews 11:36-40).]

Read *Psalm 73:1-20.*

6. What does this passage tell you about the prosperity of the wicked, and how should this impact your attitude toward them?

[The psalmist was envious and questioned why the wicked prospered. Godliness didn't seem to pay off. Then the Lord revealed the wicked person's end—sudden, eternal punishment.]

* *Facilitator*, you should have about **one hour** of class time remaining.

Day Four (Children & Taxes)

Read *Deuteronomy 6:6-7; Proverbs 22:6* and *Ephesians 6:4.*

1. According to these passages, who is responsible for teaching children how to handle money from a biblical perspective?

[Parents are responsible for teaching their children God's ways of living, including how to handle money.]

2. How well were you prepared to manage money when you first left home as a young person?

3. Describe how you would train children to:

- Budget

- Give

- Save

- Spend wisely

Read *Matthew 5:25-26* and *Romans 13:1-7.*

4. Does the Lord require us to pay taxes to the government? Describe your attitude toward paying taxes and does it need to change?

[God requires us to pay taxes because He instituted government to serve people. The consequence of tax evasion is punishment.]

Day Five (Contentment & Lifestyle)

Read *Philippians 4:11-13* and *1 Timothy 6:6-8.*

1. What do these passages say about contentment?

Philippians 4:11-13– [Contentment is not something that occurs naturally; it is learned. We can learn to be content in any circumstance.]

1 Timothy 6:6-8– [Godliness with contentment is a means of great gain. We can't take anything with us when we die, and we should be content with our basic needs satisfied.]

2. How does our culture discourage contentment, and how do you plan on practicing it?

Read *Acts 4:32-37* and *1 Thessalonians 4:11-12.*

3. What do these passages communicate to you about lifestyle?

Acts 4:32-37 — [An equality of needs being met within the body of Christ led to revival.]

1 Thessalonians 4:11-12 — [We are encouraged to live quiet, industrious lives.]

4. How do the following factors influence your present spending and lifestyle?

- Comparing your lifestyle with that of friends and others –

- Internet, television, shopping, catalogs and advertisements –

- Your study of the Bible –

- Your commitment to Christ and to things that are important to Him –

5. Do you sense that the Lord would have you change your spending or any part of your standard of living? If so, what?

Day Six (the Notes)

Read the Crisis & Perspective Notes on pages 201-223.

1. What was the most helpful concept you learned from the notes, and how will you apply it?

2. Do you sense the Lord would have you alter your lifestyle in any way? If so, in what way?

3. I will take the following *action* as a result of this week's study:

Remaining Agenda

1. __________ (10 minutes) Play the Week 8 segment of the *Navigating Your Finances* DVD.
2. __________ (10 minutes) Note in the Prayer Log requests and answers to prayers.
3. __________ (5 minutes) End in prayer.

CRISIS & PERSPECTIVE NOTES

Please read *after* completing Day 5 homework.

In this chapter, we will explore how to function God's way in a crisis, and the Lord's perspective on a variety of practical issues: lifestyle, prosperity, teaching children about money, taxes, partiality and litigation.

CRISIS

There was a knock at the door, and Bev and I glanced at each other. Would he be all we had dreamed?

We raced for the door, threw it open, and there he was. Tiny, gorgeous, and absolutely precious. Four-day-old Andrew, the baby we hoped to adopt, captured our hearts the moment we held him in our arms.

Several months later, we began to suspect that Andrew might have some physical challenges. Tragically, his birth mother had been addicted to powerful narcotics during her pregnancy, and the doctors discovered he had been born with only a fraction of his brain.

It was a very difficult time for us— emotionally, physically, and financially. Andrew required multiple surgeries. Because he suffered constant pain, he required around-the-clock care, which led to Bev's exhaustion and almost a complete physical breakdown.

Some challenges build slowly and can be anticipated; others appear without warning. Some are resolved quickly; others are chronic. Some reflect the consequences of our actions; others are completely beyond our control. Some crises impact an entire nation; others are isolated to us as individuals.

A job loss, major illness, birth of a special-needs child, business reversal, death of a family member, identity theft, military deployment of a breadwinner, home foreclosure, bankruptcy, divorce, or worldwide financial crisis can exert major pressure on us and our finances. Surveys reveal that many marriages simply don't survive the stress of these difficulties.

I call these challenges the "storms of life." While some of the storms amount to little more than a blustery rain shower, others feel like a category-five hurricane.

Please remember this one thing: No matter what the crisis, you don't face it alone. Jesus Christ is with you every step of the way.

Put yourself in the sandals of a few of God's people in the Bible who faced terrifying category-five storms. Job—in a matter of just a few hours—lost his children, his financial resources, and ultimately his health. Joseph was sold into slavery and thrown into prison. Moses and the children of Israel faced annihilation by Egypt's powerful army at the Red Sea. Daniel was tossed into the lions' den. Paul was beaten, stoned, and left for dead on his missionary journeys. The list goes on and on.

Although storms are often emotional, scary, and painful, if we maintain God's perspective, we can survive and even grow through such dark days (and nights!).

GOD'S ROLE

When facing a crisis, *nothing* is more important than knowing who God is—His love, care, control, and power. Only the Bible reveals the true extent of God's involvement in our challenges. If we have an inadequate or warped view of God and His purposes, then we won't fully embrace and learn from our challenges. What's more, we will forfeit the peace, contentment, and even joy that God makes available to us in the midst of the storm.

GOD LOVES YOU.

First John 4:8 sums up God's very nature: *"God is love."* God loves you and throughout your whole life remains intimately involved with you as an individual. Psalm 139:17 reveals, *"How precious are your thoughts concerning me, O God! How vast is the sum of them! Were I to count them, they would outnumber the grains of sand."* In other words, the Creator of the universe is always thinking about you!

When you think about it, John 15:9 has to be one of the most encouraging verses in all of the Bible. Jesus says: *"As the Father has loved me, so I have loved you."* Don't skim over those words! Let the implications sink in for a moment. Consider how much God the Father loves God the Son. They have existed forever in the closest possible relationship with a deep, unfathomable love for each other. And Jesus says this is how much He loves you!

In any crisis, it's critical to be reminded of God's unfailing love and faithfulness. Why? Because it's so very easy to become discouraged and even lose hope in such times. It's easy to forget God's love and care for you, especially when adversity first strikes—or goes on and on for what feels like an eternity.

Jeremiah the prophet was completely discouraged. He wrote: *"I remember my affliction and my wandering, the bitterness...and my soul is downcast within me"* (Lamentations 3:19-20). But then he remembered the Lord, *"Yet I call this to mind and therefore have hope. Because of the Lord's great love we are not consumed, for his compassions never fail. They are new every morning; great is your faithfulness"* (Lamentations 3:21-23).

It is helpful to meditate on passages such as these: *"God has said, 'Never will I leave you; never will I forsake you.' So we can say with confidence, 'The Lord is my helper; I will not be afraid. What can man do to me?'"* (Hebrews 13:5-6). *"Who shall separate us from the love of Christ? Shall trouble or hardship or persecution or famine or nakedness or danger or sword? ...No, in all these things we are more than conquerors through him who loved us"* (Romans 8:35, 37).

I've discovered that even in a crisis, the Lord will do kind things that offer clear evidence of His love and care for us. Consider Joseph. While a slave, "[Joseph's] *master saw that the Lord was with him"* (Genesis 39:3), so his master put him in charge of all he owned. Later in prison, *"the LORD was with Joseph and extended kindness to him, and gave him favor in the sight of the chief jailer"* (Genesis 39:21).

GOD IS IN CONTROL.

As we studied earlier, God is ultimately in control of every event. This is but a sampling of passages that affirm His control: *"Our God is in the heavens; He does whatever He pleases"* (Psalm 115:3). *"We adore you as being in control of everything"* (1 Chronicles 29:11, TLB). *"Whatever the Lord pleases, He does, in heaven and in earth"* (Psalm 135:6). *"My* [the Lord's] *purpose will stand, and I will do all that I please"* (Isaiah 46:10). *"For nothing will be impossible with God"* (Luke 1:37).

The Lord is in control even of difficult events. *"I am the Lord, and there is no other, the One forming light and creating darkness, causing well-being and creating calamity; I am the Lord who does all these"* (Isaiah 45:6-7).

GOD HAS A PURPOSE FOR ADVERSITY.

The Cecropia moth emerges from its cocoon only after a long, exhausting struggle to free itself. A young boy, wishing to help the moth, carefully slit the exterior of the cocoon. Soon it came out, but its wings were shriveled and couldn't function. What the boy didn't realize was that the moth's struggle to liberate itself from the cocoon was essential to develop its wings—and its ability to fly.

Much like the cocoon of the Cecropia moth, adversity has a part to play in our lives as well. God uses those difficult, sometimes heartbreaking times to mature us in Christ. James 1:2-4 says it this way: *"Consider it pure joy, my brothers, whenever you face trials of many kinds, because you know that the testing of your faith develops perseverance. Perseverance must finish its work so that you may be mature and complete, not lacking anything."*

God designs challenging circumstances for our ultimate benefit. Romans 8:28-29 tells us, *"We know that in all things God works for the good of those who love him, who have been called according to his purpose. For those God foreknew he also predestined to be conformed to the likeness of his Son...."* And the primary good that God works in our lives is to make us more like Christ.

We see this same thought expressed in Hebrews 12:6, 10-11, *"For those whom the Lord loves He disciplines....God disciplines us for our good, that we may share in his holiness. All discipline for the moment seems not to be joyful but sorrowful; yet to those who have been trained by it, afterwards it yields the peaceful fruit of righteousness."* God makes no mistakes. He knows exactly what He wants us to become, and also knows exactly what is necessary to produce that result in our lives.

Alan Redpath captures this truth: "There is nothing—no circumstances, no trouble, no testing—that can ever touch me until, first of all, it has gone past God, past Christ, right through to me. If it has come that far, it has come with great purpose, which I may not understand at the moment. But as I refuse to become panicky, as I lift my eyes to Him and accept it as coming from the throne of God for some great purpose of blessing to my own heart, no sorrow will ever disturb me, no trial will ever disarm me, no circumstance will cause me to fret, for I shall rest in the joy of what my Lord is."

Bev and I have endured—and benefited from—many storms. The one surrounding Andrew's birth, with most of his brain missing, until his death 11 years later drew us much closer to each other and to the Lord. Through the crucible of our pain and tears, many of the Bible's truths grew from wispy theory into rock-solid reality. We began to grasp how deeply God loved and cared for Andrew. And for us. Although we would never want to repeat this experience, we are incredibly grateful for how the Lord used it in our lives.

Author Ron Dunn observed:

> "If God subtracted one pain, one heartache, one disappointment from my life, I would be less than the person I am now, less the person God wants me to be, and my ministry would be less than He intends."

Please don't miss this point. You and I need to recognize difficulties as opportunities to grow into the people God wants us to be. In adversity, we learn things we just couldn't learn any other way.

I know what you're thinking.... "Easy for you to say, Howard. You have no idea what we've been through." Granted. But then, I could also say, "You have no idea what *we* have been through during our 40 years of marriage." And yet the Lord Jesus has stood with us in every crisis, every heartache, every difficult decision. Every one of those incidents, painful as they were, brought us closer to Him and closer to each other.

You can be comforted knowing that your loving heavenly Father is in absolute control of every situation you will ever face. He intends to use each circumstance for a good purpose. First Thessalonians 5:18 says it well, *"Give thanks in all circumstances, for this is God's will for you in Christ Jesus."*

TRUSTING GOD

We should view crises through the lens of God's love, faithfulness and control.

When Bev reached the point of total exhaustion in serving baby Andrew, we knew it would be physically impossible for us to care for him on our own. Desperately needing to rest and recover, we decided to admit him for a time to a facility that specialized in caring for profoundly handicapped children.

This was a deeply emotional time, and we openly wept in the admittance room. Then I looked up and noticed a painting of Jesus hanging on the wall. When I looked at the picture, it helped me reflect on His faithfulness, and I experienced peace. When I looked away and thought only of the circumstances, my tears flowed. In that moment, I experienced the reality of Isaiah 26:3: *"You will keep him in perfect peace whose mind is steadfast* [on You], *because he trusts in you."*

The Bible makes it clear that God offers security only in Himself—not in money, not in possessions, not in a career, and not in other people. External things offer the illusion of security, but the Lord alone can be fully trusted. *"The LORD is good, a refuge in times of trouble. He cares for those who trust in him"* (Nahum 1:7, NIV). *"When I am afraid, I will trust in you. In God, whose word I praise, in God I trust; I will not be afraid"* (Psalm 56:3-4).

THE EYE OF THE STORM

There are several things we can do to survive—and even grow—when we find ourselves in the storm.

GET YOUR FINANCIAL HOUSE IN ORDER.

I've been close to many people facing gut-wrenching financial storms. And the first question they usually ask is, How can I solve the problem?

Jesus answers the question this way in Matthew 7:24-25: *"Everyone who hears these words of mine and* ***puts them into practice*** *is like a wise man who built his house on the rock. The rain came down, the streams rose, and the winds blew and beat against that house; yet it did not fall, because it had its foundation on the rock"* (emphasis added).

The key to solving your financial problems is learning and applying God's way of handling money. It truly is that simple. That's why this study is so important.

When you finish this class, you will know God's framework for managing money. But *knowing* is only half of what you need. The other half is *applying* what you have learned.

It may take a long time and a lot of effort to navigate the storm, but you will know the basics of what you should do.

Part of what you've learned is to be a generous giver. When facing a financial crisis, the tendency is to hold on tightly to what we have and become less generous. A passage in the book of Acts, however, shows us a different way. In Acts 11:28-29 we read: *"Agabus* [a prophet]...*through the Spirit predicted that a severe famine would spread over the entire Roman world. (This happened during the reign of Claudius.) The disciples, each according to his ability, decided to provide help for the brothers living in Judea."*

Think about this. The Holy Spirit revealed through a prophet that a severe famine was coming soon, and their first reaction was to get out their checkbooks! Don't allow a crisis or a pending crisis to stop you from remaining generous. You may not be able to give as much as you did previously, but still give.

It's also important to quickly evaluate how the circumstance will impact your finances, and to make the necessary adjustments for any diminished income or increased expenses. And don't forget to communicate! Tell the Lord, and if you are married, tell each other your feelings and concerns. How important is this? It's important enough to schedule a time *every day* to share, so you can encourage each other. Bev and I discovered that a crisis doesn't have to damage our marriage; in fact, it can be a catalyst to improve it. I am fully persuaded that God intends married couples to grow closer together during a crisis rather than allowing the difficulties to damage their marriage.

NEVER GO THROUGH A STORM ALONE.

Without repeating the advice in the "Counsel" chapter, I want to emphasize the importance of not going it alone. It is almost impossible to make the wisest decisions in isolation when experiencing a crisis.

Seek advice from people who have been through similar situations. You will draw strength not only from their emotional support, but also from their experience. There are people all around you who have weathered serious life storms, and you can gain from their knowledge, learning mistakes to avoid and resources that can help. Ask your church and friends to pray; it's their most powerful contribution.

LIVE ONE DAY AT A TIME.

Robert Johnson built an extraordinarily successful construction business from scratch. He was extremely generous and enjoyed a wonderful reputation. And then came the crushing financial crisis of 2008—crippling his business and pushing him to the brink of bankruptcy.

Confiding in me one day, Robert said, "In a crisis, the tendency is to look ahead and become overwhelmed with all the problems. We are to plan ahead, but for our mental and emotional health we must follow what Jesus Christ told us: *"...do not worry about tomorrow; for tomorrow will worry about itself. Each day has enough trouble of its own"* (Matthew 6:34, NIV).

Live focused on today! And if the crisis becomes severe, focus on one moment at a time in close fellowship with Christ. This is not "escape from reality"; rather, it is a practical way to stay close to the only One who can help us through the challenge.

BE PATIENT, WAITING FOR GOD'S TIMING.

Expectations can be damaging during a crisis. When we assume that the Lord will solve our problems in a certain way by a certain time, we set ourselves up for disappointment and frustration.

Someone described patience as accepting a difficult situation without giving God a deadline for removing it. Remember, God's primary purpose in allowing a crisis in the first place is to conform you to Jesus Christ. He is at work in your life, and knows exactly how long it will take to produce the results He wants. Ecclesiastes 3:1 says, *"There is an appointed time for everything. And there is a time for every event under heaven."*

The late Larry Burkett used to say with a smile, "God is seldom early, but He's never late." Be patient. Be careful not to set deadlines for the Lord to act.

Work diligently to solve your own problems, with the recognition that you need the moment-by-moment help and counsel of the Lord who loves you. Philippians 4:6-7 is one of my favorite Bible passages when facing difficulties. Every phrase is loaded with meaning. *"Be anxious for nothing but in everything by prayer and supplication with thanksgiving let your request be made known to God and the peace of God which surpasses all understanding will guard your heart and mind in Christ Jesus."*

FORGIVE OTHERS.

Imagine you are a teenager, deeply loved by your father. Your siblings sell you into slavery, and for the next 13 years, you are a slave and a prisoner. Amazingly, on one unbelievable day, you find yourself elevated to second in command of the world's most powerful nation. Several years later, your starving siblings—the ones who betrayed you—beg you for food. What's your response: retaliation or forgiveness?

This is the question Joseph had to answer, and he forgave. How was he able to do this? Because he recognized that God had orchestrated his circumstances—even the ones that were so deeply traumatic and painful. *"God sent me ahead of you…"* he told his brothers, *"to save your lives by a great deliverance. So then, it was not you who sent me here, but God"* (Genesis 45:7-8).

God realizes how critical it is for us to forgive those who are involved in causing our crisis, regardless of their motivation. One of the most impressive characteristics of Jesus Christ was His willingness to forgive. Imagine hanging on a cross in excruciating agony, and at the same time praying for those who had crucified you: *"Father, forgive them for they do not know what they are doing"* (Luke 23:34).

When the apostle Peter asked Jesus if he should forgive someone seven times, He responded, *"not seven times, but seventy-seven times"* (Matthew 18:22, NIV). He then told a parable about a servant who was forgiven a large debt by his master but refused to forgive a fellow servant a small debt. Christ describes what happens to the unforgiving servant: *"In anger his master turned him over to the jailers to be tortured until he should pay back all he owed. This is how my heavenly Father will treat each of you unless you forgive your brother from the heart"* (Matthew 18:34, NIV).

In order to grow more like Christ and experience the benefits He intends for us during a crisis, we must forgive. And more than forgive, we are to be kind, compassionate, and seek to be a blessing.

"Be kind and compassionate to one another, forgiving each other, just as in Christ, God forgave you (Ephesians 4:32).

"Not returning evil for evil, or insult for insult, but giving a blessing instead; for you were called for the very purpose that you might inherit a blessing" (1 Peter 3:9).

Unforgiveness can be a daily battle, particularly if the crisis has been horribly hurtful. But it harms the person who refuses to forgive. My wife, Bev, describes it as swallowing poison and hoping the other person will die. When we refuse to forgive, the bitterness in our heart can turn toxic, consuming our thoughts and eating away our emotional health. Forgiveness and seeking to bless the other person, however, lead to freedom.

It is imperative to pray regularly for the Lord to give us the desire to forgive, and then to give us His love for the people who may have harmed us. Jesus tells us also to pray for them, *"Love your enemies and pray for those who persecute you, that you may be sons of your Father in heaven"* (Matthew 5:44). It's hard to remain bitter toward someone for whom you are praying regularly.

COMMON CHALLENGES

Let's examine two of the most common financial challenges people face.

Job loss

Losing your job ranks among life's most stressful events—not just for you, but for your spouse as well if you are married. Meet together and discuss ways to minimize the emotional and financial toll on both of you. And encourage each other because often a job loss is a blessing in disguise. God may bring you a better career opportunity, and it can build your faith as you experience His providing your needs even without a job.

Next, formulate a game plan for the job search—from drafting a resume to networking with friends. *When you lose a job, your **full-time** job should be finding a new job.*

In addition to cutting back on spending for discretionary items, there are two financial goals to keep in mind. First, make every effort to avoid using debt for living expenses. Many people mask the real situation by using debt to fund current spending. Make good, hard decisions not to spend one penny you don't have to. Every borrowed penny must be repaid *with interest,* and although spending it is easy, repayment is always hard work.

Second, do what you can to maintain health insurance. You may be able to assume your health insurance coverage through a plan from your former employer. If not, get advice from others on cost-efficient coverage.

Illness or accident

If you suffer a major illness or accident, it's a double whammy. Medical expenses pile on as income plunges. If the condition is severe enough to prevent future employment, you will need to make permanent adjustments. And if either health insurance or disability coverage is inadequate, it can be financially catastrophic.

If married, be prepared for the possibility that one of you may need to make important decisions without the benefit of input from the other. Bev and I have decided that if one of us is seriously ill, the other will make the financial and health-related decisions. We are each familiar with the location of all important records and know how to use them.

Don't be embarrassed to make your needs known to your family, friends, and church. Extend to them the opportunity to help meet your needs. Giving to those in need is a big part of what it means to follow Christ. Galatians 6:2 reminds us, *"Carry each other's burdens, and in this way you will fulfill the law of Christ."*

PREPARING FOR FUTURE STORMS

You can't prevent every difficulty, but you can prepare to survive them by building a solid relationship with the Lord—and your spouse, if you are married—and by improving your finances. The healthier your finances, the better you will be able to cope. Proverbs 27:12 says, *"The prudent see danger and take refuge, but the simple keep going and suffer for it."*

The more time you spend getting to know God and what He reveals in the Bible—and applying what you've learned—the better prepared you will be to weather life's storms.

One of the biggest benefits of making progress on your journey to true financial freedom is that it provides a financial margin when you find yourself facing an unexpected crisis. By the time Andrew was born, we had paid off all our debts including the mortgage. Even though we were debt-free at the time, we knew that his medical expenses would be a challenge. And they were. Our freedom from debt, however, helped us to focus on Andrew and each other as we dealt with his problems.

LIFESTYLE

The Bible doesn't demand one standard of living for everyone. In Scripture, godly people are represented in all walks of life, and the Lord continues to place His people strategically in every level of society—rich and poor. We encourage you to evaluate your standard of living. To stimulate your thinking, let's examine several scriptural principles that should influence your lifestyle.

1. LEARN TO BE CONTENT.

First Timothy 6:8 issues this challenging statement: *"And if we have food and covering* [clothes and shelter], *with these we shall be content."* Our culture has restated this verse to read, "If you can afford the finest food, wear the latest fashions, drive the newest luxury automobile, play with all the most up-to-date electronic gadgets, and live in a beautiful home, then you will be happy." Our consumption-oriented society operates on the assumptions that more is always better, and that happiness is based on acquiring.

The word "contentment" is mentioned six times in Scripture, and five times it has to do with money. Paul wrote, *"I have learned to be content in whatever circumstances I am. I know how to get along with humble means, and I also know how to live in prosperity; in any and every circumstance I have learned the secret of being filled and going hungry, both of having abundance and suffering need. I can do all things through Him who strengthens me"* (Philippians 4:11-13).

Take note that Paul "learned" to be content. It wasn't automatic. It wasn't a slam dunk. Contentment didn't suddenly show up after Paul received Christ as his Savior. The fact is none of us are born intuitively content; rather, we learn contentment.

There are three elements to the secret of contentment:

- Knowing what God says about handling money
- Practicing what God says about it
- Then trusting God to provide exactly what He knows is best

Note carefully that it's not just knowing these things that brings contentment; it's *doing* them. Once we have been faithful in the doing, we can be content in knowing that our loving heavenly Father will entrust the precise possessions He knows will be best for us at any particular time—whether much or little. Biblical contentment is not to be equated with laziness or apathy. Because we serve a dynamic God, Christians should work hard. Contentment does not exclude properly motivated ambition. In fact, I believe we should have a burning desire to be increasingly faithful stewards of everything entrusted to us.

Biblical contentment is an inner peace that accepts what God has chosen for our present vocation, station in life, and financial situation.

Hebrews 13:5 emphasizes this: *"Let your way of life be free from the love of money, being content with what you have; for He Himself has said, 'I will never desert you, nor will I ever forsake you.'"*

2. COMPARING YOUR LIFESTYLE TO OTHERS' IS DANGEROUS.

Some use comparison to justify spending more than they should. Many have suffered financially because they tried—but could not afford—to "keep up with the Joneses." Someone once said, "You can never keep up with the Joneses. Just about the time you've caught them, they go deeper in debt to buy more stuff!" If you are wealthy, your lifestyle should be based on the conviction that the Lord wants you to have a certain standard of living, and not one necessarily dictated by the maximum you can afford.

3. ENJOY WHAT GOD GIVES YOU THE FREEDOM TO BUY.

Prayerfully submit spending decisions to the Lord. Seeking the Lord's direction in spending doesn't mean we will never spend for anything other than basic necessities. During one Christmas season, my wife asked me to purchase a kitchen appliance that I considered extravagant. However, I promised to seek the Lord's direction. As we prayed, He made it clear that we should purchase the appliance, which we thoroughly enjoyed. *"For everything created by God is good, and nothing is to be rejected, if it is received with gratitude"* (1 Timothy 4:4).

4. MAKE AN EFFORT TO LIVE SIMPLY.

Every possession requires time and often money to maintain, and they can demand so much time or money that they distract us from our relationships with the Lord and our families. A quiet, simple life—with adequate time to invest in our most important relationships—is the safest environment for any marriage or family. As 1 Thessalonians 4:11-12 says, *"Make it your ambition to lead a quiet life and attend to your own business and work with your hands, just as we commanded you; so that you may behave properly toward outsiders and not be in any need."*

Simply don't allow yourself to become unduly encumbered with the cares of this life. *"Suffer hardship with me, as a good soldier of Christ Jesus. No soldier in active service entangles himself in the affairs of everyday life, so that he may please the one who enlisted him as a soldier"* (2 Timothy 2:3-4).

5. WEALTH IS MEANINGLESS APART FROM SERVING JESUS CHRIST.

King Solomon, the author of Ecclesiastes, had an annual income of more than $35 million. He lived in a palace that took thirteen years to build, and owned 40,000 stalls of horses. The daily menu of his household included a 100 sheep and 30 oxen.

Obviously, Solomon was in a position to know whether money would bring true fulfillment. He concluded, *"Vanity of vanities…all is vanity!"* (Ecclesiastes 12:8). *Nothing*, even extraordinary success, can replace the value of our relationship with the Lord. Ask yourself this question: Am I sacrificing a close relationship with Christ in the pursuit of wealth? *"For what does it profit a man to gain the whole world, and forfeit his soul?"* (Mark 8:36).

6. DON'T BE CONFORMED TO THIS WORLD.

Romans 12:2 says, *"Do not be conformed to this world—this age, fashioned after and adapted to its external, superficial customs"* (Romans 12:2, Amplified). We live in the most affluent culture in the history of the world, where we are constantly bombarded with costly, manipulative advertising to prompt us to spend money. Advertisers usually stress the importance of image rather than function. For example, automobile ads rarely focus on a car as reliable, economic transportation. Instead, they project an image of status or sex appeal.

No matter what the product—clothing, deodorants, credit cards, you name it—the message is communicated that the *fulfilling, beautiful, wrinkle-free life* can be ours if we are willing to buy it. Unfortunately, to some extent this media onslaught has influenced all of us. Author George Fooshee so aptly states,

"People buy things they do not need with money they do not have to impress people they do not even like."

POVERTY, PROSPERITY OR STEWARDSHIP?

Some Christians embrace one of two extremes. On one end of the spectrum are those who believe that godliness can only occur in poverty. We learned earlier that a number of godly people in Scripture were among the wealthiest of their day. In the Old Testament, the Lord extended the reward of abundance to the children of Israel when they were obedient, while the threat of poverty was one of the consequences of disobedience. Deuteronomy 30:15-16 reads, *"I have set before you today life and prosperity, and death and adversity; in that I command you today to love the LORD your God, to walk in His ways and to keep His commandments...that the LORD your God may bless you."*

We may legitimately pray for prosperity when our relationship with the Lord is healthy and we have a proper perspective of possessions. *"Beloved, I pray that in all respects you may prosper and be in good health, just as your soul prospers"* (3 John 2). The Bible doesn't say that a godly person must live in poverty.

At the other end of the spectrum lies the belief that all Christians who truly have faith will always prosper. This extreme is also in error. Joseph is an example of a faithful person who experienced prosperity and poverty. He was born into a prosperous family, then was thrown into a pit, and sold into slavery by his jealous brothers. While Joseph was a slave, his master promoted him to be head of his household. Later he made the righteous decision not to commit adultery with his master's wife, yet was thrown in jail because of that decision—and held there for several years! In God's timing, however, he was ultimately elevated to Prime Minister of Egypt.

Look at a graph of Joseph's life:

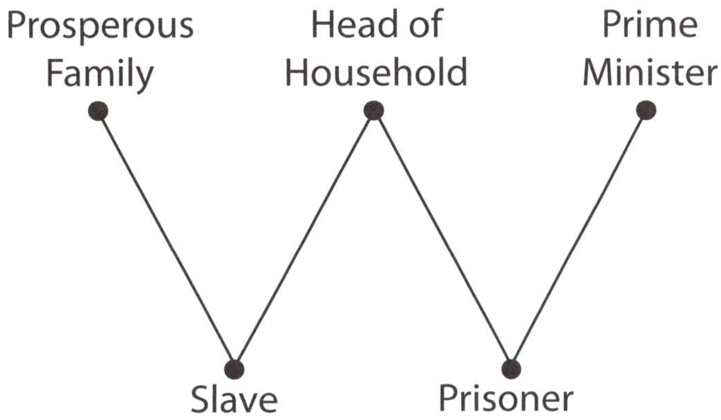

The guideline for prosperity is found in Joshua 1:8, *"This book of the law shall not depart from your mouth, but you shall meditate on it day and night so that you may be careful to do according to* ***all*** *that is written in it; for then you will make your way prosperous, and then you will have success"* (emphasis added).

Two requirements for prosperity become apparent from studying this passage. You must meditate on the Scriptures, engraving them on your mind and heart, and you are required to do all that is written in them. Once you have fulfilled these obligations, you place yourself in the position to be blessed financially. But there is no guarantee that the godly will *always* experience financial prosperity. There are four reasons why the godly may not prosper:

1. VIOLATING SCRIPTURAL PRINCIPLES

Look again at Joshua 1:8. There is the requirement to do according to *all* that is written in the Bible. You may be giving generously but acting dishonestly. You may be honest but not fulfilling your work responsibilities. You may be a faithful employee but head over heels in debt. One of the biggest benefits of this study is that we explore what the entire Bible teaches about money. Those who don't understand all the requirements often neglect critical areas of responsibility unknowingly, and suffer financially.

2. BUILDING GODLY CHARACTER

Romans 5:3-4 reads, *"Tribulation brings about perseverance, and perseverance, proven character."* Many godly people in the Bible went through periods when they were living righteously, yet lost their possessions. David became a national hero after slaying Goliath. Here was a young man who served blamelessly, only to be forced to flee for his life from a tormented King Saul. Job lost his children and possessions in the space of a few moments, yet was described as a *"blameless and upright man, fearing God and turning away from evil"* (Job 1:8). Paul learned the secret of contentment while being held captive in chains and suffering want, even though he was righteous.

God sometimes molds our character by allowing us to experience difficult circumstances. An example of how the Lord develops character in a people before prospering them is found in Deuteronomy 8:16-18: *"In the wilderness He fed you manna which your fathers did not know, that He might humble you and that He might test you, to do good for you in the end. Otherwise, you may say in your heart, 'My power and the strength of my hand made me this wealth.' But you shall remember the LORD your God, for it is He who is giving you power to make wealth."* The children of Israel needed to be humbled before they could handle wealth. Our Father knows us better than we know ourselves. In His infinite wisdom, He knows exactly how much He can entrust to us at any time without it harming our relationship with Him.

3. OUR DEPENDENCE

A father was carrying his two-year-old child as he waded out into a lake. When they were close to shore, the child was unconcerned because of the apparent safety of the beach—even though the water was deep enough to drown him. He didn't understand his dependence upon his father. The farther they moved away from shore, however, the tighter the child held to his father. Like the child, we are *always* completely dependent upon the Lord to provide for us. However, often we don't recognize our dependence when we are "close to shore," experiencing the apparent security of financial prosperity. But when our possessions are few or none, it's easier to recognize our need and to cling to our heavenly Father.

4. THE MYSTERY OF GOD'S SOVEREIGNTY

In Hebrews 11, we find "Faith's Hall of Fame." In verses 1-35, we encounter a list of people who triumphed miraculously by the exercise of their faith in God. But in verse 36, the writer directs our attention to godly people who gained God's approval, yet experienced poverty. God ultimately chooses how much to entrust to each person, and sometimes we simply can't understand His decisions.

Let's summarize: The Scriptures neither teach the necessity of poverty, nor promise uninterrupted prosperity. What the Bible teaches is the responsibility of being a faithful steward through all the ups and downs of life. Please review this diagram, which contrasts the three perspectives.

	Poverty	Stewardship	Prosperity
Possessions are:	Evil	A responsibility	A right
I work to:	Meet only basic needs	Serve Christ	Become rich
Godly people are:	Poor	Faithful	Wealthy
Ungodly people are:	Wealthy	Unfaithful	Poor
I give:	Because I must	Because I love God	To get
My spending is:	Without gratitude to God	Prayerful and responsible	Carefree and consumptive

Before we leave the issue, it's important for us to understand the Lord's perspective of prosperity. The Lord evaluates true riches based on His spiritual value system, which is stated most clearly in Revelation. The godly poor are rich in God's sight. *"I* [the Lord] *know your tribulation and your poverty (but you are rich)"* (Revelation 2:9). Those who are wealthy, yet do not enjoy a close relationship with Christ, are actually poor. *"Because you say, 'I am rich, and have become wealthy, and have need of nothing,' and you do not know that you are wretched and miserable and poor and blind and naked"* (Revelation 3:17).

The bottom line? True prosperity extends far beyond material possessions. True prosperity is gauged by how well we know Jesus Christ and by how closely we follow Him.

DANGERS OF PROSPERITY

Scripture identifies a number of dangers associated with wealth. First, wealth tends to separate people. Abram and Lot were relatives who became wealthy. This ultimately caused them to move away from each other. *"Now Abram was very rich in livestock, in silver and in gold...*[Lot] *also had flocks and herds and tents. And the land could not sustain them while dwelling together; for their possessions were so great that they were not able to remain together"* (Genesis 13:2, 5-7). Most of us know friends or family members who have allowed conflicts over money to damage or destroy their relationships.

Second, it's easy for those who are prosperous to turn from God. We might say to ourselves, "That would never happen to me." But Scripture makes it clear that an increase in possessions and wealth moves us closer to spiritual danger. *"For when I* [the Lord] *bring them into the land flowing with milk and honey, which I swore to their fathers, and they have eaten and are satisfied and become prosperous, then they will turn to other gods and serve them, and spurn Me"* (Deuteronomy 31:20).

Third, it's difficult for the rich to come to know Jesus Christ as their Savior. *"Jesus said to His disciples, 'Truly I say to you, it is hard for a rich man to enter the kingdom of heaven'"* (Matthew 19:23). Again, this is because the rich generally feel less of a need for God. Riches also can destroy a spiritually fruitful life. *"The one on whom seed was sown among the thorns, this is the man who hears the word, and the worry of the world, and the deceitfulness of riches choke the word, and it becomes unfruitful"* (Matthew 13:22). Riches are deceitful because they are tangible and can blind us from the reality of the unseen Lord. We imagine that our finances can do things for us that only Christ can really do.

TEACHING CHILDREN

In 1904, the country of Wales experienced a remarkable revival. Thousands of people were introduced to Christ, and the results were dramatic. Bars closed because of lack of business. Policemen exchanged their weapons for white gloves, since crime disappeared. Wales was so evangelically minded that it sent missionaries all over the world.

One of those missionaries traveled to Argentina, where on the streets he led a young boy to Christ. The boy's name was Luis Palau. He has since become known as the "Billy Graham" of Latin America. Palau visited Wales to express his thankfulness for helping lead him to Christ. What he discovered was astonishing. Less than one-half of one percent of the Welsh attended church. Divorce was at an all-time high, and crime was increasing.

As a result of this experience, Palau produced a film titled *God Has No Grandchildren*. The thrust of the film is that each generation is responsible for passing on the truths of Scripture, including God's financial principles, to its children. Proverbs 22:6 reads,

"Train up a child in the way he should go, even when he is old he will not depart from it."

Parents should be *MVP* parents. MVP is an acronym that describes the three methods to teach children God's way of handling money: *Modeling, Verbal communication,* and *Practical opportunities.* All three are needed to train your children. Let's look at each.

MODELING

Since children soak up parental attitudes toward money like a sponge soaks up water, parents must model handling money wisely. Paul recognized the importance of modeling when he said, *"Be imitators of me, just as I also am of Christ"* (1 Corinthians 11:1).

Luke 6:40 is a challenging passage. It reads, *"Everyone, after he has been fully trained, will be like his teacher."* Another way of saying this is that we can teach what we believe, but we only reproduce who we are. There is no substitute for parents being good models.

VERBAL COMMUNICATION

Parents need to tell their children *why* they are handling money the way they are. The Lord charged the Israelites, *"These words, which I am commanding you today, shall be on your heart. You shall teach them diligently to your sons and shall talk of them when you sit in your house and when you walk by the way and when you lie down and when you rise up"* (Deuteronomy 6:6-7). We must verbally instruct children in the ways of the Lord, but children need more than a good example and verbal instruction; they also need practical experience.

PRACTICAL EXPERIENCE

Teaching money management must be done by parents and not delegated to teachers because spending experiences are found outside the classroom. Consider five areas where this is possible:

1. Income

As soon as children are ready for school, they should begin to receive an income to manage. Parents need to decide whether the child must earn an income, or if they wish to give an allowance in return for the child doing chores.

The amount of the income will vary according to factors such as the child's age, the ability to earn, and the financial circumstances of the family. The amount, however, isn't as important as the responsibility of handling money. At first, as with any new experience, the child will make many mistakes. When this happens, don't hesitate to let the "law of natural consequences" run its course. Yes, you will be tempted to help when the child spends all the income the first day on an unwise purchase. *But don't bail the child out!* Mistakes will be the best teacher.

Parents should establish boundaries and offer advice on how to spend money, but your child must have freedom of choice within those boundaries. Every Saturday I used to bicycle to the store with my son, Matthew, to buy him a pack of gum. Despite my advice, the entire pack would be consumed that day.

Later, we decided that Matthew would have to buy his own gum. I will never forget the expression on his face as he came out of the store with his first purchase. "This gum cost me *all* my money!" he yelled. That pack of gum lasted all week.

2. Budgeting

When children start to receive an income, teach them to budget. Begin with a simple system consisting of three jars, labeled separately: GIVE, SAVE, and SPEND. The child distributes a portion of the income into each jar. Even a six-year-old can understand this method because when there's no more money to spend, the spend jar is empty!

When children become teenagers, they should begin using a written budget—or train them to use one of the budgeting software or online programs that are available. During the training, teach shopping skills, the ability to distinguish needs from wants, and the importance of waiting on the Lord to provide. Warn them about the danger of impulse spending.

One valuable lesson you can teach children is to seek the Lord's provision through prayer. We often rob ourselves of this opportunity by buying things or charging purchases without praying for the Lord to supply them.

One couple asked their son to pray for some shirts he needed. Later, a friend in the clothing business asked if their son needed shirts, because he had excess inventory. They excitedly responded, "Yes!" Their friend brought 10 shirts to their home. That evening as their son began to pray for his shirts, the father said, "You don't have to pray for those shirts. God has answered your prayers." They brought the shirts out one by one. By the tenth shirt, their son thought God was in the shirt business.

3. Saving and investing

The habit of saving should begin as soon as the child receives an income. It's helpful to open a savings account in the child's name. As children mature, expose them to various types of investments: stocks, bonds, etc. Also, teach children the benefits of compounding interest. If they grasp this concept and become faithful savers, they will enjoy financial stability as adults. Parents should demonstrate this by saving for something that will directly benefit the children. Use a graph the children can fill in so they can visually chart the progress of saving.

Children should have both short-term and long-term saving goals. The younger the child, the more important are short-term goals. To a four-year-old, a week seems like a lifetime to save for a purchase. They won't understand saving for their future education, but will get excited about saving for a small toy.

4. Debt

Also teach how difficult it is to get out of debt. A father loaned his son and daughter money to buy bicycles. He drew up a credit agreement with a schedule for repayment of the loan. After they went through the long process of paying off the loan, the family celebrated with a "mortgage burning" ceremony. The children appreciated those bikes more than any of their possessions, and decided to avoid debt in the future.

5. Giving

The best time to establish the habit of giving is when you're young. It's helpful for children to give a portion of their gifts to a need they can *see*. For example, a child understands when the gift helps to buy food for a needy family he actually knows.

Richard Halverson, the late U.S. Senate chaplain, gave his son, Chris, this heritage as a child. Chris gave money to support Kim, an orphan who had lost his sight during the Korean War. Chris was taught to feel that Kim was like an adopted brother. One Christmas, Chris bought Kim a harmonica. Kim cherished this gift from Chris and learned to play it well. As the years went by, Kim became an evangelist, and his presentation of the gospel included playing the harmonica.

When your child is a teenager, serving at the local homeless shelter or taking a mission trip to a Third World country can be a powerful experience. Exposure to poverty can initiate a lifetime of giving to the needy. We also recommend a family time each week for dedicating that week's gifts to the Lord.

LEARNING EXPERIENCES IN MONEY MAKING

Parents also have a responsibility to train children to develop work habits. If children learn how to work with the proper attitude, they will have taken a giant step toward becoming a valuable commodity in the job market. There are three areas to consider in this training:

1. Learning routine responsibilities

The best way for a child to become a faithful worker is to establish the habit of daily household chores. These are tasks that each member of the family is expected to perform.

2. Expose children to your work

Many children really have no idea how their father or mother earns an income. An important way to teach the value of work is to expose children to the parents' means of making a living.

One word of advice: Because most children are no longer with their parents at work, parents' work habits around the home will be a major influence. If a parent works hard away from home, but complains about washing the dishes at home, what's being communicated to the children? Examine your work activities at home to ensure that you are properly influencing them.

3. Working for others

Baby-sitting, bagging groceries, or waiting on tables will be an education. A job gives a child an opportunity to enter into an employee-employer relationship and to earn extra money. The objective of teaching children the value of work is to build character. A working child with the proper attitude will be a more satisfied individual. He or she will grow up with more respect for the value of money and the effort required to earn it.

SINGLE PARENTS AND GRANDPARENTS

Single parents are increasingly common, and if you are one, we appreciate the added demands you face. But be encouraged. Some of the most responsible children I have ever met have been raised by a godly single mother or father. We pray God will honor your efforts.

If you are a grandparent, you have a wonderful opportunity to influence your grandchildren. We recommend that the parents meet with the grandparents and together design a strategy for training the grandchildren how to handle money. It's important for grandparents to play a role in which they complement the objectives of the parents. Too often parents and grandparents have not reached agreement on how to train the next generation. This can lead to bruised relationships and ineffective training.

STRATEGY FOR INDEPENDENCE

Finally, establish a strategy for independence. Lyle and Marge Nelsen have four amazingly responsible children. They have had each child managing all of his or her own finances (with the exception of food and shelter) by the senior year in high school. Following this course, Lyle and Marge stayed available to advise the children as they learned—through successes and failures—to make good spending decisions.

As the people of Wales discovered, God has no grandchildren. Passing on our faith in Christ to the next generation can be compared to a relay race. Any track coach will tell you that relays are won or lost in the passing of the baton from one runner to another. Seldom is the baton dropped once it's firmly in the grasp of a runner. If it's going to be dropped at all, it will most likely happen in the exchange between the runners. Adults have the responsibility to pass the baton of practical biblical truths to the younger generation. May our generation leave our children the blessed legacy of financial faithfulness.

WHY DO THE WICKED PROSPER?

The prophet Jeremiah inquired of the Lord: *"You are always righteous, O Lord, when I bring a case before you. Yet I would speak with you about your justice: Why does the way of the wicked prosper?"* (Jeremiah 12:1, NIV). This is a disturbing question God's people have asked for centuries.

The author of Psalm 73 also asked why the wicked prospered, and he admitted being envious of them. Then the Lord revealed the wicked person's end—sudden eternal punishment. *"Surely God is good to…those who are pure in heart. But as for me, my feet had almost slipped…for I envied the arrogant when I saw the prosperity of the wicked.… When I tried to understand all this, it was oppressive to me till I entered the sanctuary of God; then I understood their final destiny. Surely you place them on slippery ground; you cast them down to ruin. How suddenly are they destroyed, completely swept away by terrors!"* (Psalm 73:1-19, NIV).

The Bible tells us that though some of the wicked will certainly prosper, we are not to envy them because life on earth is short. *"Do not fret because of evil men or be envious of those who do wrong; for like the grass they will soon wither, like green plants they will soon die away"* (Psalm 37:1-2, NIV). We are to maintain the Lord's perspective and His eternal value system.

PARTIALITY

Study carefully James 2:1-9: *"My brethren, do not hold your faith in our glorious Lord Jesus Christ with an attitude of personal favoritism. For if a man comes into your assembly with a gold ring and dressed in fine clothes, and there also comes in a poor man in dirty clothes, and you pay special attention to the one who is wearing the fine clothes…have you not made distinctions among yourselves, and become judges with evil motives? …If, however, you are fulfilling the royal law, according to the Scripture, 'You shall love your neighbor as yourself,' you are doing well.*

But if you show partiality, you are committing sin and are convicted by the law as transgressors."

Through the years, I have found myself struggling with this sin of partiality. Far more often than I would care to admit, this has unintentionally influenced my actions. Once when I hung up the phone, my wife said, "I know you weren't talking to Ken. It must have been Ryan. You like Ken better, and it shows in your voice."

Partiality doesn't have to be based on a person's wealth. It can also be based on a person's education, social position, or spiritual status. James 2:9 could not be more blunt: *"But if you show partiality, you are committing sin and are convicted by the law as transgressors."* How do we break the habit of partiality? Romans 12:10 tells us, *"Be devoted to one another in brotherly love; give preference to one another in honor."* And Philippians 2:3 reads, *"With humility of mind let each of you regard one another as more important than himself."*

We need to ask the Lord to ingrain in our thinking the habit of consciously elevating each person, regardless of his or her station in life, as more important than ourselves.

TAXES

What does the Bible say about paying taxes?

That's the same question that was asked of Jesus. *"Is it lawful for us to pay taxes to Caesar or not?...* [Jesus] *said to them, 'Show Me a* [Roman coin]. *Whose likeness and inscription does it have?' And they said, 'Caesar's.' And He said to them, 'Then give to Caesar the things that are Caesar's...'"* (Luke 20:22-25).

Some people will tell you to avoid paying taxes at any cost. After all, they will reason, look how much the government wastes and squanders. But the Bible tells us to pay our taxes. *"Let every person be in subjection to the governing authorities. For there is no authority except from God, and those which exist are established by God...because of this you also pay taxes, for rulers are servants of God, devoting themselves to this very thing. Render to all what is due them: tax to whom tax is due"* (Romans 13:1, 6-7). It's certainly permissible to reduce taxes by using legal tax deductions, but we should be careful not to make unwise decisions simply to avoid paying taxes.

LITIGATION

Suing seems to be a national pastime: A woman sued a man who she said kicked her at a nightclub. She sought $200,000 as compensation for the injury and lost time on the dance floor.

There are a number of reasons for this flood of lawsuits, including an avalanche of new laws, and more disturbing than that is the stark fact that people are becoming less and less forgiving. The court system uses an adversarial process, which frequently creates animosities between the parties involved. Instead of trying to heal, the system provides a legal solution—but leaves the problems of toxic unforgiveness and anger untouched.

The Bible stresses that the goal should be reconciliation. *"If therefore you are presenting your offering at the altar, and there remember that your brother has something against you, leave your offering there before the altar, and go your way; first be reconciled to your brother"* (Matthew 5:23-24).

Scripture states that when Christians are at odds with one another, they should not settle their disputes through the courts. *"Does any one of you, when he has a case against his neighbor, dare to go to law before the unrighteous, and not before the saints? Or do you not know that the saints will judge the world? And if the world is judged by you, are you not competent to constitute the smallest law courts? Do you not know that we shall judge angels? How much more, matters of this life? If then you have law courts dealing with matters of this life, do you appoint them as judges who are of no account in the church? I say this to your shame. Is it so, that there is not among you one wise man who will be able to decide between his brethren, but brother goes to law with brother, and that before unbelievers? Actually, then, it is already a defeat for you, that you have lawsuits with one another. Why not rather be wronged? Why not rather be defrauded?"* (1 Corinthians 6:1-7).

Instead of initiating a lawsuit, a three-step procedure for Christians to resolve their differences is set forth in Matthew 18:15-17: *"If your brother sins, go and reprove him in private; if he listens to you, you have won your brother. But if he does not listen to you, take one or two more with you, so that by the mouth of two or three witnesses every fact may be confirmed. And if he refuses to listen to them, tell it to the church; and if he refuses to listen even to the church, let him be to you as a Gentile and a tax-gatherer."*

1. GO IN PRIVATE. The party who believes he has been wronged needs to confront the other person in private with his claims. If the dispute remains unresolved, then:

2. GO WITH ONE OR TWO OTHERS. The person who feels wronged should return with witnesses who can confirm facts or help resolve the dispute. If this is still unsuccessful, then:

3. GO BEFORE THE CHURCH. The third step is mediation or arbitration before an impartial group in the church, or perhaps a Christian conciliation service, if this is available in your area.

The greatest benefit of following this procedure is not simply reaching a fair settlement of the dispute, but practicing forgiveness and demonstrating love.

LET'S GET PRACTICAL!

ORGANIZING YOUR ESTATE

Someone once said that people will work 40 years to accumulate assets, about 10 years conserving what they've accumulated, but no more than two hours planning for its ultimate distribution. Approximately seven out of ten people die without a will. Dying without a will has four major drawbacks.

1. The state laws will dictate who receives your assets. For instance, in some states a wife would receive only one-third to one-half of the husband's estate, with the children (even adult children) receiving the rest.
2. The heirs will face more cumbersome court proceedings and added legal fees.
3. The estate may pay higher estate taxes than would have been paid with wise planning.
4. Tragically, under some circumstances, the court can appoint a guardian (who may not know the Lord) to raise your children.

The person who knows Christ has a solemn duty to provide for his family. *"But if anyone does not provide for his own, and especially for those of his household, he has denied the faith, and is worse than an unbeliever"* (1Timothy 5:8). This requirement extends to the responsibility of planning for the future of your loved ones should you predecease them.

Whether you are married or single, rich or poor, you should have a will or trust and complete the Organizing Your Estate worksheet. As Isaiah told Hezekiah,

"Thus says the Lord, 'Set your house in order, for you shall die'" (2 Kings 20:1).

Someday you will die. One of the greatest gifts you can leave your loved ones for that emotional time will be an organized estate. Thirty-six percent die before retirement. So do not delay in preparing your will just because you are young. An increasingly popular option to the traditional will is a revocable living trust. Please seek legal and tax counsel before you decide which instrument is most suitable for you to use.

Complete the Organizing Your Estate worksheet, and review the information with your spouse or heirs. After the review, give a completed copy to your attorney or accountant and a trusted family member or friend who will be involved in settling your estate.

The Organizing Your Estate worksheet is designed to be brief and is not intended to fully organize your estate. We strongly recommend that you enroll in the Set Your House In Order small group study to more thoroughly organize your estate.

MEETING WITH YOUR ATTORNEY

It will save you time and money if you are prepared to meet with your attorney to draft your will. Make these decisions in advance: (1) who will be my personal representative, and who will be the successor personal representative of my estate, (2) who will be the guardian and successor guardian of our children, (3) who are my heirs, and what will each of them receive, and (4) how much do I want to give from my estate to the Lord's work.

It will also save time if you bring your personal financial statement with you.

ORGANIZING YOUR ESTATE

Date: January 15, 2011

WILL AND/OR TRUST

The Will (Trust) is located: David Smart's office

The person designated to carry out its provisions is: Janet

If that person cannot or will not serve, the alternate is: James faithful

Attorney: David Smart Phone: (555) 321-1000

Accountant: Jennifer Numbers Phone: (555) 432-4000

INCOME BENEFITS

1. Company Benefits

My (our) heirs will receive the following company benefits: One-third regular wage

Contact: HR Department Phone: (555) 786-4545

2. Social Security Benefits

To receive Social Security benefits, go to the Orlando, florida Social Security office.
Do this promptly because a delay may void benefits. When you go, take: (1) my Social Security card; (2) my death certificate; (3) your birth certificate; (4) our marriage certificate; (5) birth certificates for each child.

3. Veterans' Benefits

You are/are not eligible for veterans' benefits: Are not

To receive these benefits, you should do the following: N/A

4. Life Insurance Coverage

Insurance company: Good Insurance Co. Policy #: 563-777

Face Value: $150,000 Person insured: Don Beneficiary: Janet

Insurance company: Solid Insurance Co. Policy #: 838-776

Face Value: $50,000 Person insured: Janet Beneficiary: Don

SAMPLE

FAMILY INFORMATION

Family member's name:

Don — Address: 12 Nice Ave., Pleasantville, OH
Social Security #: 123-45-6789

Janet — Address: 12 Nice Ave., Pleasantville, OH
Social Security #: 234-56-7890

John — Address: 12 Nice Ave., Pleasantville, OH
Social Security #: 345-67-8901

Ruth — Address: 12 Nice Ave., Pleasantville, OH
Social Security #: 456-78-9012

________ Address: ________
Social Security #: ________

________ Address: ________
Social Security #: ________

MILITARY SERVICE HISTORY

Branch of Service: Navy   Service number: 9876543

Length of Service: 3 years   From: 5/17/95   Until: 4/20/99

Rank: First Class (E-6)

Location and description of important military documents: Honorable discharge in the cabinet at home

FUNERAL INSTRUCTIONS

Funeral Home: King's Funeral

Address: 325 Orange St., Orlando, Florida   Phone: (555) 645-3000

My (our) place of burial is located at: Wood Lawn Memorial Gardens

I (we) request burial in the following manner: A closed casket

I (we) request that memorial gifts be given to the following church/organization:

First Church — Address: 400 Main St., Orlando

Food for the Poor Ministries — Address: 200 Second Ave., Orlando

SAMPLE

ORGANIZING YOUR ESTATE

Date: ____________________

WILL AND/OR TRUST

The Will (Trust) is located: ____________________

The person designated to carry out its provisions is: ____________________

If that person cannot or will not serve, the alternate is: ____________________

Attorney: ____________________ Phone: ____________________

Accountant: ____________________ Phone: ____________________

INCOME BENEFITS

1. Company Benefits

My (our) heirs will receive the following company benefits:____________________

Contact: ____________________ Phone: ____________________

2. Social Security Benefits

To receive Social Security benefits, go to the ____________________Social Security office.

Do this promptly because a delay may void benefits. When you go, take: (1) my Social Security card; (2) my death certificate; (3) your birth certificate; (4) our marriage certificate; (5) birth certificates for each child.

3. Veterans' Benefits

You are/are not eligible for veterans' benefits: ____________

To receive these benefits, you should do the following: ____________________

____

4. Life Insurance Coverage

Insurance company: ____________________ Policy #: ____________

Face Value: __________ Person insured: __________ Beneficiary: ____________

Insurance company: ____________________ Policy #: ____________

Face Value: __________ Person insured: __________ Beneficiary: ____________

FAMILY INFORMATION

Family member's name:

______________________ Address: ______________________
Social Security #: ______________________

______________________ Address: ______________________
Social Security #: ______________________

______________________ Address: ______________________
Social Security #: ______________________

______________________ Address: ______________________
Social Security #: ______________________

______________________ Address: ______________________
Social Security #: ______________________

______________________ Address: ______________________
Social Security #: ______________________

MILITARY SERVICE HISTORY

Branch of Service: ______________ Service number: ______________

Length of Service: ______________ From: __________ Until: __________

Rank: ______________________

Location and description of important military documents: ______________________

____

FUNERAL INSTRUCTIONS

Funeral Home: ______________________________________

Address: ______________________________ Phone: ______________

My (our) place of burial is located at: ______________________

I (we) request burial in the following manner:______________________

I (we) request that memorial gifts be given to the following church/organization:

______________________ Address: ______________________

______________________ Address: ______________________

CRISIS BUDGET

The best time to prepare a budget for a crisis is *before* one happens because you are not under emotional stress. An added benefit is that it often helps people reduce unnecessary spending *now*.

Review your current budget and ask this question: If I (we) were in a crisis that demanded reduced spending, what cuts would be made? Consider trying to reduce your spending by a certain percentage, such as ten or twenty percent.

REDUCE OR ELIMINATE THESE EXPENSES

Expenses	Describe Reduction	Amount Reduced
Cable TV	Discontinue cable	$ 25.00
Electricity	Be more careful with it	35.00
Water	Be more careful with it	5.00
Car payment	Sell car and buy used for cash	200.00
Gas & Oil	Drive less	40.00
Eating out	Discontinue most eating out	100.00
Vacation	Reduce time away	25.00
Pets	Give away fish and hamsters	5.00
Clothing	Buy less clothing and buy 2nd hand	40.00
Savings	Cut in half	80.00
Allowances	Reduce	30.00
Subscriptions	Discontinue	20.00
Gifts	Cut in half	25.00

Total Amount Reduced: $630

Percentage Reduced: (divide amount reduced by total budget expenses) 15%

SAMPLE

CRISIS BUDGET

REDUCE OR ELIMINATE THESE EXPENSES

Expenses	Describe Reduction	Amount Reduced

Total Amount Reduced: ____________

Percentage Reduced: (divide amount reduced by total budget expenses) ____________

TRACK & TWEAK

Continue to track your income and spending on pages 186-187, and note below any new tweaks you decide to start.

TWEAK SHEET

What to Tweak	Spending Reduced	Income Increased
________________________________	__________	__________
________________________________	__________	__________
________________________________	__________	__________
________________________________	__________	__________
________________________________	__________	__________
________________________________	__________	__________
________________________________	__________	__________
________________________________	__________	__________
________________________________	__________	__________
________________________________	__________	__________

9

ETERNITY

FACILITATORS GUIDE

"For what does it profit a man to gain the whole world, and forfeit his soul?" (Mark 8:36).

"When we've been there ten thousand years,
Bright shining as the sun,
We've no less days to sing God's praise
Than when we'd first begun"
—*Amazing Grace,* **by John Newton (1725-1807)**

ETERNITY

Facilitators Guide for Week 9

Let's Get Practical!

☐ Continue **Tracking & Tweaking** your budget or visit the Money Lounge online.

☐ Complete your **Financial Goals** on pages 253-259.

☐ **Share your Compass experience** and give us advice on how to improve the Navigating course by logging on to **compass1.org**, click on Small Group Studies Tools & Resources and then click on the Navigating Study Student and Facilitator Tools.

Agenda

1. __________ (5 minutes) Open in prayer.

2. __________ (5 minutes) Everyone individually recites from memory:

"For what does it profit a man to gain the whole world, and forfeit his soul?" (Mark 8:36)

3. __________ (85 minutes) Begin the group discussion.

Reminder

Encourage everyone to complete their Navigating story and share suggestions to improve the study by logging on to **compass1.org** "click on Small Group Studies Tools & Resources and then click on the Navigating Study Student and Facilitator Tools.

Day One (Financial goals)

Complete your Financial Goals on pages 253-259.

1. Do you have any questions about your Financial Goals?

2. What did you learn that was especially helpful, and how will you apply it?

3. What changes in your lifestyle will you make in light of your goals?

Day Two (Life is short)

Read *Psalm 39:4-6* and *Psalm 103:13-16.*

1. What do these passages say to you about the length of life on earth?

[Life on earth is very short.]

Read *Psalm 90:10, 12.*

2. Why do you think that Moses suggested numbering your days?

[Numbering our remaining days on earth helps us realize the brevity of our lives, so we are better able to make wise decisions on how to use our time and money.]

3. Estimate the number of days you have left on earth. How does this impact your thinking?

4. Based on your number of days, what actions will you take?

Day Three (My identity)

Read *1 Chronicles 29:15; Philippians 3:20* and *1 Peter 2:11.*

1. What do these passages say about your identity on earth and in heaven?

1 Chronicles 29:15—[We are aliens, strangers, and sojourners on earth.]

Philippians 3:20—[We are citizens of heaven, which is our real home.]

1 Peter 2:11—[We are strangers on this earth.]

Read *2 Peter 3:10-13.*

2. In the future, what will happen to the earth?

[The earth and everything on it will be completely destroyed.]

3. How will this impact the way you invest your time and spend your money?

* *Facilitator*, you should have about **one hour** of class time remaining.

Day Four (Judgment)

Read *Ecclesiastes 12:13-14* and *2 Corinthians 5:9-10.*

1. What will happen to each of us in the future?

Ecclesiastes 12:13-14—[The Lord will judge all of our actions, even those we think are hidden.]

2 Corinthians 5:9-10—[All of us will stand before the judgment seat of Christ and give an account of our deeds.]

Read *1 Corinthians 3:11-15.*

2. How would you describe the works (give some examples) that will be burned at this final judgment?

[Any action done out of what the Bible calls the flesh—anything done apart from submission to Christ as Lord—will be burned. This includes anything done out of pride or with improper motives.]

3. Give some examples of works that will be rewarded.

[The smallest deed, when done to glorify Christ, will be rewarded. In Matthew 10:42, the Lord tells us that even giving someone a cup of water will be rewarded.]

4. What are you doing that will survive this final judgment?

Day Five (Eternity)

Read *2 Corinthians 4:18.*

1. What does this verse say to you?

[What we see will last only a relatively short time. The things we cannot see will last forever and should be of primary importance to us.]

2. As you reflect on eternity, answer these questions thoughtfully: What three things do I want to accomplish during the rest of my life?

3. What can I do during my lifetime that would contribute most significantly to the cause of Christ?

4. In light of these answers, what actions or changes do I need to make?

Day Six (the Notes)

Read the Eternity Notes on pages 241-252.

1. What was the most important concept you learned from reading the notes?

2. How will you apply this to your life?

3. Describe what has been the most beneficial part of the Small Group Study for you, and why.

Remaining Agenda

1. __________ (10 minutes) Play the Week 9 segment of the *Navigating Your Finances* DVD.

2. __________ (5 minutes) Take long-term prayer requests, and note them on the Prayer Logs.

3. __________ (5 minutes) Facilitators, pray for each participant individually.

Reminder

Facilitators, we suggest you write each class member (or couple) an encouraging letter, e-mail or text message summarizing what you appreciate most about them.

May the Lord richly bless you in every way for serving others.

ETERNITY NOTES

Please read *after* completing Day 5 homework.

On Monday, October 25, 1999, the news reported an unfolding story. Air Force jets following a Learjet from Orlando, Florida, were unable to communicate with its pilots. I learned later that two very close friends, Robert Fraley and Van Ardan, were on that Lear as it carried them and golfer Payne Stewart to their deaths.

One of the most critical principles for us to understand when handling money is the reality of eternity. Robert and Van were men in their mid-forties who lived with an eternal perspective. Robert had framed these words in his workout area, "Take care of your body as though you will live forever; take care of your soul as if you will die tomorrow."

Because God loves us, He reveals in the Bible that there is a heaven and hell, that there is a coming judgment, and that He will grant eternal rewards. The Lord wants the very best for us. For this reason, He wants to motivate us to invest our lives and finances in such a way that we can enjoy an intimate relationship with Him now—and receive the greatest possible rewards and responsibilities in the life to come.

Our failure to view our present lives through the lens of eternity is one of the biggest hindrances to seeing our lives and our finances in their true light. Yet Scripture states that the reality of our eternal future should determine the character of our present lives and the use of our money and possessions.

People who don't know the Lord look at life as a brief interval that begins at birth and ends at death. Looking to the future, they see no further than their own life span. With no eternal perspective, they think, *If this life is all there is, why deny myself any pleasure or possession?*

Those who know Christ have an entirely different perspective. We know life is short; it's the preface—not the book; it's the preliminary—not the main event. And yet this brief testing period will determine much of our experience in heaven.

Financial planners try to convince people to look down the road instead of simply focusing on today. "Don't think in terms of this year," they will tell you. "Think and plan for 30 years from now." The wise person does indeed think ahead, but far more than 30 years ahead. More like 30 *million* years ahead. Someone once said, "He who provides for this life but takes no care for eternity is wise for a moment but a fool forever." Jesus said it this way: *"What does it profit a man to gain the whole world, and forfeit his soul?"* (Mark 8:36).

THE LONG AND SHORT OF IT

The Bible frequently reminds us that life on earth is brief: "[God] *is mindful that we are but dust"* (Psalm 103:14). Our earthly bodies are called *"tents"* (2 Peter 1:13, NIV), temporary dwelling places of our eternal souls. David recognized this and sought to gain God's perspective on the brevity of life. He asked of the Lord, *"Show me, O Lord, my life's end and the number of my days; let me know how fleeting is my life.... Each man's life is but a breath. Man is a mere phantom...he heaps up wealth, not knowing who will get it"* (Psalm 39:4-6, NIV).

When a friend discovered she had only a short time to live, she told me of her radical change in perspective. "The most striking thing that's happened," she said, "is that I find myself almost totally uninterested in accumulating more things. Things used to matter to me, but now I find my thoughts are centered on Christ, my friends, and other people."

Do we have to be facing death to gain such a perspective? If that's the case, then we ought to think often on the words of Hebrews 9:27: *"It is appointed for men to die once and after this comes judgment."* We all have our "appointed time" to step out of this life and into eternity.

Moses realized that true wisdom flowed out of understanding that our lives are short. With that in mind, he asked the Lord to help him number the days he had on earth.

"As for the days of our life, they contain seventy years, or if due to strength, eighty years...for soon it is gone and we fly away.... So teach us to number our days, that we may present to You a heart of wisdom" (Psalm 90:10, 12).

I encourage you to number the days you estimate that you have left on earth. If I live as long as my father, I have about 6,000 days left. This has helped me become aware that I need to invest my life and resources in efforts that will count for eternity.

When I served in the Navy, I was very interested in the town in which I was stationed. Things changed, however, as soon as I received orders discharging me in two months. I became what was called a "short-timer." My interest completely shifted from the town I was leaving to the town that would become my new home. In a similar way, when we realize that we are really "short-timers" on earth and will soon be going to our real home, our focus will shift to what is important in heaven. Author Matthew Henry said, "It ought to be the business of every day to prepare for our last day."

ETERNITY IS LONG

Eternity, on the other hand, *never ends*. It is forever. Imagine a cable running through the room where you are now. To your right, the cable runs billions of light years all the way to the end of the universe; to your left, it runs to the other end of the universe. Now imagine that the cable to your left represents eternity past, and the cable to your right, eternity future. Place a small mark on the cable in front of you. That tiny mark represents your brief life on earth.

Because most people don't have an eternal perspective, they live as if the mark were all there is. They make *mark* choices, live in *mark* houses, drive *mark* cars, wear *mark* clothes, and raise *mark* children. Devotional writer A.W. Tozer referred to eternity as "the long tomorrow." This is the backdrop against which all the questions of life and the handling of our resources must be answered.

ALIENS AND PILGRIMS

Scripture tells us several things about our identity and role on earth. First, *"Our citizenship is in heaven"* (Philippians 3:20), not earth. Second, *"We are ambassadors for Christ"* (2 Corinthians 5:20), representing Him on earth. Imagine yourself as an ambassador working in a country that is generally hostile to your own. Naturally, you want to learn about this new place, see the sights, and become familiar with the people and culture. But suppose you eventually become so assimilated into this foreign country that you begin to regard it as your true home. Your allegiance wavers, and you gradually compromise your position as an ambassador, becoming increasingly ineffective in representing the best interests of your own country.

We must never become too much at home in this world, or we will become ineffective in serving the cause of the kingdom we are here to represent. We are aliens, strangers, and pilgrims on earth. Peter wrote, *"Live your lives as strangers here in reverent fear"* (1 Peter 1:17, NIV). Later he added, *"I urge you, as aliens and strangers in the world, to abstain from sinful desires"* (1 Peter 2:11, NIV). Another Bible translation uses the words *"strangers and pilgrims"* (KJV).

Pilgrims are unattached. They are travelers—not settlers—aware that the excessive accumulation of things can distract. Material things are valuable to pilgrims, but only as they facilitate their mission. Things can entrench us in the present world, acting as chains around our legs that keep us from moving in response to God. When our eyes are too focused on the visible, they will be drawn away from the invisible. *"So we fix our eyes not on what is seen, but on what is unseen. For what is seen is temporary, but what is unseen is eternal"* (2 Corinthians 4:18, NIV).

Pilgrims of faith look to the next world. They see earthly possessions for what they are: useful for kingdom purposes, but far too flimsy to bear the weight of trust. Thomas à Kempis, author of *The Imitation of Christ,* said it this way: "Let temporal things serve your use, but the eternal be the object of your desire." Two principles concerning possessions help us gain a proper perspective of them.

1. WE LEAVE IT ALL BEHIND.

After wealthy John D. Rockefeller died, his accountant was asked how much he left. The accountant responded, "He left it all."

Job said it this way: *"Naked I came from my mother's womb, and naked I shall return there"* (Job 1:21). Paul wrote,

> *"We have brought nothing into the world, so we cannot take anything out of it either"* (1 Timothy 6:7).

The psalmist observed, *"Do not be afraid when a man becomes rich…for when he dies he will carry nothing away; his glory will not descend after him. Though while he lives he congratulates himself—and though men praise you when you do well for yourself—he shall go to the generation of his fathers"* (Psalm 49:16-20).

2. EVERYTHING WILL BE DESTROYED.

Earthly goods won't last forever; they are destined for annihilation. *"The day of the Lord will come like a thief. The heavens will disappear with a roar; the elements will be destroyed by fire, and the earth and everything in it will be laid bare. Since everything will be destroyed in this way, what kind of people ought you to be? You ought to live holy and godly lives"* (2 Peter 3:10-11, NIV). Understanding the temporary nature of possessions should influence us as we consider spending decisions.

JUDGMENT

It's uncomfortable to think about judgment. But because our Lord loves us so deeply, He wants us to realize what will happen in the future. For this reason, God revealed to us that we all will be judged according to our deeds: *"He has fixed a day in which He will judge the world in righteousness"* (Acts 17:31). All of us should live each day with this awareness: *"They will have to give an account to Him who is ready to judge the living and the dead"* (1 Peter 4:5, NIV).

God will judge us with total knowledge: *"Nothing in all creation is hidden from God's sight. Everything is uncovered and laid bare before the eyes of Him to whom we must give account"* (Hebrews 4:13,

NIV). Because His knowledge is total, His judgment is comprehensive: *"Men will have to give account on the day of judgment for every careless word they have spoken"* (Matthew 12:36, NIV). His judgment extends to what is hidden from people. *"God will bring every deed into judgment, including every hidden thing, whether it is good or evil"* (Ecclesiastes 12:14, NIV). He will even *"disclose the motives of men's hearts"* (1 Corinthians 4:5).

The Bible teaches that all those who do not know Christ will be judged and sent to an indescribably dreadful place. *"I saw a great white throne and Him who was seated on it...and I saw the dead, great and small, standing before the throne.... Each person was judged according to what he had done... If anyone's name was not found written in the book of life, he was thrown into the lake of fire"* (Revelation 20:11-15, NIV). The good news is that you can know Christ.

YOU CAN KNOW GOD

I was 28 years old when I started attending a breakfast with several young businessmen. It wasn't long before I was impressed by their business savvy. But more than that, I was attracted by the quality of their lives. I didn't know what they had, but whatever it was, I wanted it.

These men spoke openly of their faith in God. I had grown up going to church, but the religion I had seen modeled during those years meant nothing to me as an adult. I had concluded it was only a fairy tale until a friend described how I could enter into a *personal* relationship with Jesus Christ. He explained several truths from the Bible I had never understood before.

GOD LOVES YOU AND WANTS YOU TO KNOW HIM.

God desires a close relationship with each of us.

"For God so loved the world, that He gave His only begotten Son, that whoever believes in Him shall not perish, but have eternal life" (John 3:16).

"I [Jesus] *came that they might have life, and have it abundantly"* (John 10:10).

When my son, Matt, was in the first grade, he had a burning desire to win the 100-yard dash at his school's field day, but unfortunately, his classmate Bobby Dike was faster.

Field day finally arrived. They ran the 50-yard dash first, and Bobby beat Matt badly. I will never forget Matt coming up to me with tears in his eyes, saying, "Dad, please pray for me in the 100-yard dash. I've just got to win." My heart sank as I nodded.

With the sound of the gun, Matt got off quickly. He pulled away from the rest of his classmates and won. I lost it, jumping and shouting with an exhilaration I had never before experienced. Then it occurred to me how much I loved my son. Although I love other people, I don't love them enough to give my son to die for them. But that is how much God the Father loves you. He gave His only Son, Jesus Christ, to die for you.

UNFORTUNATELY, WE ARE SEPARATED FROM GOD.

God is holy—which simply means God is perfect, and He can't have a relationship with anyone who is not perfect. My friend asked if I had ever sinned—done anything that would disqualify me from perfection. "Many times," I admitted. He explained that every person has sinned, and the consequence of sin is separation from God. *"All have sinned and fall short of the glory of God"* (Romans 3:23). *"Your sins have cut you off from God"* (Isaiah 59:2, TLB).

GOD'S ONLY PROVISION TO BRIDGE THIS GAP IS JESUS CHRIST.

Jesus Christ died on the cross to pay the penalty for our sin, bridging the gap between God and us. Jesus said, *"I am the way, and the truth, and the life; no one comes to the Father but through Me"* (John 14:6). *"God demonstrates His own love towards us, in that while we were yet sinners, Christ died for us"* (Romans 5:8).

This diagram illustrates our union with God through Jesus Christ:

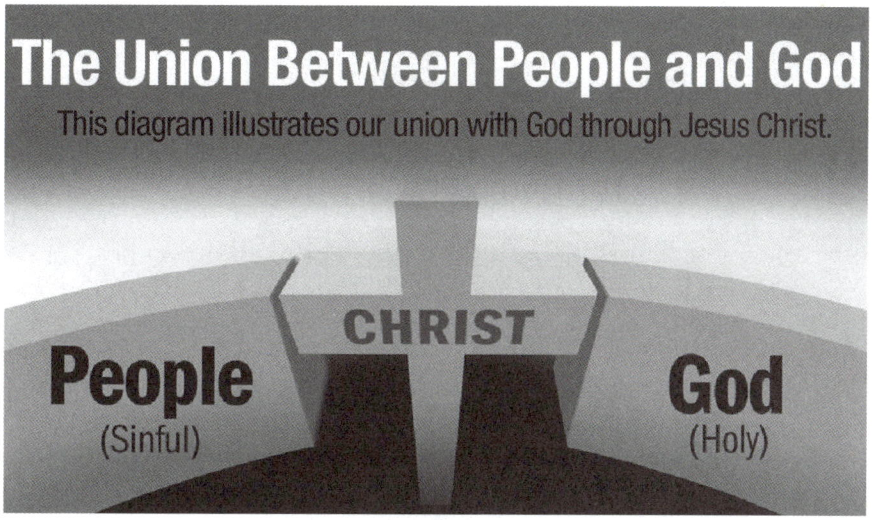

THIS RELATIONSHIP IS A GIFT FROM GOD.

My friend explained that by faith I could receive the free gift of a relationship with God. The transaction appeared unfair. I had learned in business that a transaction happens only when both sides are convinced they are getting more than they are giving up. But now I was being offered a relationship with God, and it was free! *"It is by grace you have been saved, through faith—this is not from yourselves, it is the gift of God—not by works, so that no one can boast"* (Ephesians 2:8-9, NIV).

I had only to ask Jesus Christ to come into my life to be my Savior and Lord. So I did! As my friends will tell you, I'm a very practical person—if something doesn't work, I stop doing it. I can tell you from more than thirty-five years of experience that a relationship with God works. And it is available to you through Jesus Christ. Nothing in life compares with knowing Christ personally. We can experience true peace, joy, and hope when we know Him. It's the only way you can enjoy *true financial freedom.*

If you want to know God and aren't certain whether you have this relationship, I encourage you to receive Jesus Christ right now. Pray a prayer similar to the one I prayed: "God, I need You. I'm sorry for my sin. I invite Jesus to come into my life as my Savior and Lord, and to make me the person You want me to be. Thank You for forgiving my sins and giving me the gift of eternal life."

You might go all the way on your financial journey, but without a relationship with Christ, it won't have any lasting value.

If you asked Christ into your life, you have made the most important decision anyone could ever make.

I urge you to find a local church that teaches the Bible, one where you can begin to learn what it means to follow Jesus Christ.

JUDGMENT OF BELIEVERS

After they die, those who know Christ will spend eternity with the Lord in heaven, an unimaginably wonderful place. But what we seldom consider is that the entry point to heaven is a *judgment.*

Scripture teaches that all believers in Christ will give an account of their lives to the Lord. *"We shall all stand before the judgment seat of God.... So then each of us will give an account of himself to God"* (Romans 14:10, 12). The result of this will be the gain or loss of eternal rewards. In 1 Corinthians 3:13-15 (NIV) we read, *"His work will be shown for what it is, because the* [Judgment] *Day will bring it to light.... If what he has built survives, he will receive his reward. If it is burned up, he will suffer loss."* Our works are what we have done with our time, influence, talents, and resources.

God's Word doesn't treat this judgment as just a meaningless formality before we get on to the real business of heaven. Rather, Scripture presents it as a monumental event in which things of eternal significance are brought to light.

MOTIVATION AND REWARDS

Why should I follow God's guidance on money and possessions when it's so much fun to do whatever I please with my resources? After all, I'm a Christian. I know I'm going to heaven anyway. Why not have the best of both worlds—this one *and* the next? Though few of us would be honest enough to use such language, these questions reflect a common attitude.

The prospect of eternal rewards for our obedience is a neglected key to unlocking our motivation. Paul was motivated by the prospect of eternal rewards. He wrote, *"I have fought the good fight, I have finished the course, I have kept the faith; in the future there is laid up for me the crown of righteousness, which the Lord, the righteous Judge, will award to me on that day"* (2 Timothy 4:7-8). Our heavenly Father uses three things to motivate us to obey Him: the love of God, the fear of God, and the rewards of God. These are the same things that motivate my children to obey me. Sometimes their love for me is sufficient motivation, but other times it isn't. In a healthy sense, they also fear me. They know I will discipline them for wrongdoing. They also know I will reward them with my words of approval and sometimes in tangible ways for doing right.

UNEQUAL REWARDS IN HEAVEN

It is not as simple as saying, "I'll be in heaven and that's all that matters." On the contrary, Paul spoke about the loss of reward as a *terrible loss,* and the receiving of rewards from Christ as a phenomenal gain. Not all Christians will have the same rewards in heaven.

John Wesley said, "I value all things only by the price they shall gain in eternity." God's kingdom was the reference point for him. He lived as he did, not because he didn't treasure things, but because he treasured the right things. We often miss something in missionary martyr Jim Elliot's famous words, "He is no fool who gives what he cannot keep to gain what he cannot lose." We focus on Elliott's willingness to sacrifice, and so we should. At the same time, however, we often overlook his motivation for gain. What separated him from many Christians was not that he didn't want treasure, but that he wanted *real* treasure. Remember, God loves you deeply. Because He wants the best for you throughout eternity, God has revealed that today's financial sacrifices and service for Him will pay off forever.

IMPACTING ETERNITY TODAY

Our daily choices determine what will happen in the future. What we do in this life is of eternal importance.

We only live on this earth once. *"It is appointed for men to die once and after this comes judgment"* (Hebrews 9:27). There is no such thing as reincarnation. Once our life on earth is over, we will never have another chance to move the hand of God through prayer, to share Christ with one who doesn't know the Savior, to give money to further God's kingdom, or to share with the needy.

Those who dabble in photography understand the effect of the "fixer." In developing a photograph, the negatives are immersed in several different solutions. The developing solution parallels this life. As long as the photograph is in the developing solution, it is subject to change. But when it is dropped in the fixer or "stop bath," it is permanently fixed, and the photograph is done. So it will be when we enter eternity: the life each of us lives on earth will be fixed as is, never to be altered or revised.

Alfred Nobel was a Swedish chemist who made a fortune by inventing dynamite and explosives for weapons. When Nobel's brother died, a newspaper accidentally printed Alfred's obituary instead. He was described as a man who became rich by enabling people to kill each other with powerful weapons. Shaken from this assessment, Nobel resolved to use his fortune to reward accomplishments that benefit humanity. We now know those rewards as the Nobel Peace Prize. Let's put ourselves in Nobel's place. Let's read our own obituary, not as written by people, but as it would be written from heaven's point of view. Then let's use the rest of our lives to edit that obituary into what we really want it to be.

I loved playing Little League baseball as a young boy. We played on a huge diamond with towering fences in the outfield. Years later, shortly after my father died, I spent the day walking around my old hometown reflecting on his life. When I visited the baseball field, I was shocked. It was so small! I could actually step over the outfield fences. While standing there, a thought struck me: many of those things that seem so large and important to us today shrink to insignificance in just a few years.

When I am face to face with Christ and look back on my life, I want to see that the things in which I invested my time, creativity, influence, and money are big things to Him. I don't want to squander my life on things that won't matter throughout eternity.

During Moses' time, Pharaoh was the most powerful person on earth. Pharaoh's daughter adopted Moses as an infant, giving him the opportunity to enjoy the wealth and prestige of a member of the royal family. Hebrews 11:24-26 tells us what Moses later chose and why. *"By faith Moses, when he had grown up, refused to be called the son of Pharaoh's daughter, choosing rather to endure ill-treatment with the people of God than to enjoy the passing pleasures of sin, considering the reproach of Christ greater riches than the treasures of Egypt; for he was looking to the reward."* Because Moses was looking forward to the only rewards that would last, he chose to become a Hebrew slave, and was used by God in a remarkable way.

What are the choices facing you now? How does an eternal perspective influence your decisions? Martin Luther said his calendar consisted of only two days: "today" and "that Day." May we invest all that we are and have today in light of *that* day.

Author **Randy Alcorn** graciously contributed some of this chapter and original concepts from his outstanding book *Money, Possessions and Eternity*. (Wheaton, IL: Tyndale Publishers, 1989, 2003.) We heartily recommend it! Visit his web site www.epm.org.

LET'S REVIEW

At the beginning of this study, we asked why the Bible says so much about money—in more than 2,350 verses. We offered four reasons:

1. How we handle money impacts our fellowship with the Lord.
2. Money is the primary competitor with Christ for the lordship of our life.
3. Money molds our character.
4. The Lord wants us to have a road map for handling money so that we can become financially faithful in very practical ways.

Review this diagram of the wheel, identifying the eight areas of our responsibilities, each with its primary thrust.

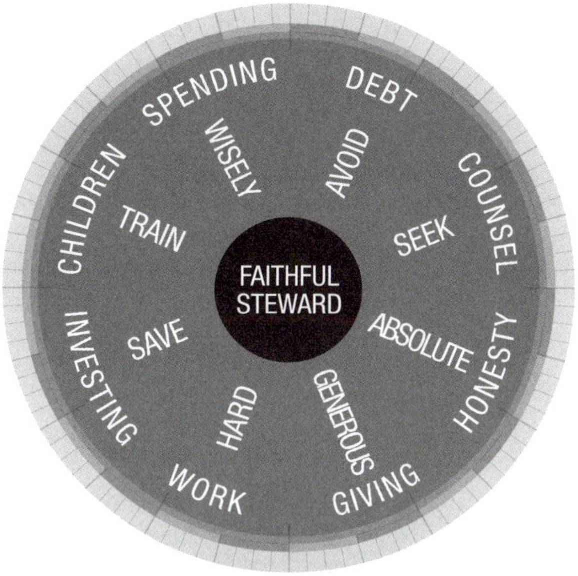

FAITHFULNESS IS A JOURNEY.

Applying the financial principles of the Bible is a journey that takes time. It's easy to become discouraged when your finances aren't completely under control by the end of this study. It takes the average person at least a year to apply most of these principles, and even longer if you have made financial mistakes. Many COMPASS graduates decide to conduct this study because they know the facilitators learn more than anyone else. As they help the others in their class, the facilitators make progress on their own journey to true financial freedom.

FAITHFULNESS IN SMALL MATTERS IS FOUNDATIONAL.

Some people become frustrated by the inability to solve their financial problems quickly. Remember, simply be faithful with what you have—be it little or much. Some abandon the goal of becoming debt-free or increasing their saving or giving because the task looks impossible. And perhaps it is—without the Lord's help. Your job is to make a genuine effort, no matter how small it may appear, and then leave the results to God. I love what the Lord said to the prophet Zechariah, *"For who has despised the day of small things?"* (Zechariah 4:10). Don't be discouraged. Be persistent. Be faithful in even the smallest matters. We have repeatedly seen the Lord bless those who tried to be faithful.

NOW IS THE TIME!

At the risk of being misunderstood by some, I want to share an experience that has fueled my passion to help people learn and apply God's way of handling money. The year was 1977, and I was in the home alone when suddenly I was overcome by the Spirit of God and found myself prostrate on the floor, weeping.

While on the floor, the Lord revealed to me that during my lifetime our nation would experience economic upheaval and a very, very difficult time. God didn't show me precisely when this will occur or what it will be like, but there is no doubt that it will happen.

The financial crisis of 2008 that engulfed the entire globe, made it clear that the economies of the world are more fragile than most people imagined. So what should you do to survive the coming economic storm?

We plead with you to become diligent in your efforts to get out of debt, give generously, budget, save and work as unto the Lord. In short, become a faithful steward. One of the best ways to demonstrate your love for your family and friends is to get your financial house in order and encourage others to do the same.

If you have a desire to help others learn God's way of handling money, we encourage you to serve as a small group facilitator. These are the heroes of COMPASS because it is in the small group where lives change most. If you wish to impact your entire church, there are opportunities to serve as a church coordinator.

We appreciate the effort you have invested in this study. And we pray this has given you a greater appreciation for the Bible, helped you develop close friendships, and above all, nurtured your love for Jesus Christ. May the Lord richly bless you on your journey to true financial freedom.

LET'S GET PRACTICAL
FINANCIAL GOALS

Determining your financial goals will help you accomplish what's important to you.

Here's how to proceed:

1. Complete the Financial Goals worksheet on page 257. If married, we suggest you and your spouse separately write down your goals, then compare them and compile a complete list on the worksheet.
2. Don't limit yourself by your current situation. Many of your goals may be "faith" goals that you must trust the Lord to provide. So pray and prioritize your goals.
3. List your goals for the coming year. One caution: Don't set completely unrealistic goals. It's better to accomplish three goals than to become frustrated with 10 unattainable ones.

FINANCIAL GOALS

Date: January 15

Giving Goals

Would like to give 15 percent of my income.

Would like to increase my (our) giving by ½ percent each year.

Other giving goals: Contribute $5,000 to world missions over the next ten years and help support one needy child

Debt Repayment Goals

Would like to pay off the following debts first:

Creditor	Amount
Visa	$ 350.00
Sears	$2,400.00
MasterCard	$4,250.00
Crazy Lou's Auto Sales	$5,000.00

Educational Goals

Would like to fund the following education:

Person	School	Annual Cost	Total Cost
John	Vo-Tech	$4,000.00	$ 8,000.00
Melissa	State College	$9,500.00	$38,000.00

Other educational goals: Michelle would like to study to become a teacher.

SAMPLE

Lifestyle Goals

Would like to make the following major purchases (home, automobile, etc.):

Item	Amount
Add Porch to Home	$8,000.00
Replace Janet's Car	$8,500.00
Replace Refrigerator	$ 900.00

Would like to achieve the following annual income: $60,000.00

Saving & Investment Goals

Would like to save 10 percent of my income.

Other saving goals: Increase savings to 15% a year within ten years

Would like to make the following investments:	Investment amount
Rental property	$25,000.00 down payment
Retirement account	$ 3,000.00 each year
Mutual fund	$ 2,000.00 each year

Would like to provide my (our) heirs with the following: House and rental property paid for and enough insurance to provide an adequate income to meet their needs

Starting a business

Would like to begin my (our) own business: Michelle would like to own her own day care facility within the next 5 years

SAMPLE

Goals For This Year

I believe the Lord wants me (us) to accomplish these goals this year:

Priority	Financial Goals	Our Part	God's Part
1	Increase Giving	Write Check	Provide Money
2	Save 10 percent	Reduce Spending	Give Wisdom
3	Pay off 2 credit cards	Sell Boat	Provide Buyer
4			
5			
6			
7			
8			
9			
10			

SAMPLE

FINANCIAL GOALS

Date: ______________

Giving Goals

Would like to give ____________ percent of my income.

Would like to increase my (our) giving by _______ percent each year.

Other giving goals: ____

____

Debt Repayment Goals

Would like to pay off the following debts first:

Creditor	Amount
______________________________	_____________
______________________________	_____________
______________________________	_____________
______________________________	_____________
______________________________	_____________

Educational Goals

Would like to fund the following education:

Person	School	Annual Cost	Total Cost
_______________	__________________	____________	____________
_______________	__________________	____________	____________
_______________	__________________	____________	____________

Other educational goals: ____

Lifestyle Goals

Would like to make the following major purchases (home, automobile, etc.)

Item	Amount
______________________________	____________
______________________________	____________
______________________________	____________

Would like to achieve the following annual income: ____________

Saving & Investment Goals

Would like to save __________ percent of my income

Other saving goals: ______________________________

Would like to make the following investments:	Investment amount
______________________________	____________
______________________________	____________
______________________________	____________

Would like to provide my (our) heirs with the following: ______________________________

____

Starting a business

Would like to begin my (our) own business: ______________________________

____

____

Goals For This Year

I believe the Lord wants me (us) to accomplish these goals this year:

Priority	Financial Goals	Our Part	God's Part
1	____________	____________	____________
2	____________	____________	____________
3	____________	____________	____________
4	____________	____________	____________
5	____________	____________	____________
6	____________	____________	____________
7	____________	____________	____________
8	____________	____________	____________
9	____________	____________	____________
10	____________	____________	____________

TRACK & TWEAK

Continue to track your income and spending on pages 186-187, and note below any new tweaks you decide to start.

TWEAK SHEET

What to Tweak	Spending Reduced	Income Increased

PRAYER LOG

Name: ______________________________

Cell Phone: ______________________________

E-Mail Address: ______________________________

Home Address: ______________________________

____

____

Home Phone: ______________________________

Spouse: ______________________________

Spouse Cell Phone: ______________________________

Spouse E-mail Address: ______________________________

Children (ages): ______________________________

____

____

____

Prayer Requests	**Answers to Prayers**
Week 1	
Week 2	
Week 3	
Week 4	
Week 5	
Week 6	
Week 7	
Week 8	

Week 9 (Long-Term Prayer Request)

____

"Pray for one another" James 5:16

PRAYER LOG

Name: ______________________________

Cell Phone: ______________________________

E-Mail Address: ______________________________

Home Address: ______________________________

____

____

Home Phone: ______________________________

Spouse: ______________________________

Spouse Cell Phone: ______________________________

Spouse E-mail Address: ______________________________

Children (ages): ______________________________

____

____

____

Prayer Requests	Answers to Prayers
Week 1	
Week 2	
Week 3	
Week 4	
Week 5	
Week 6	
Week 7	
Week 8	

Week 9 (Long-Term Prayer Request)

____

"Pray for one another" James 5:16

PRAYER LOG

Name: ______________________________ Spouse: ______________________________

Cell Phone: ______________________________ Spouse Cell Phone: ______________________________

E-Mail Address: ______________________________ Spouse E-mail Address: ______________________________

Home Address: ______________________________ Children (ages): ______________________________

______________________________ ______________________________

______________________________ ______________________________

Home Phone: ______________________________ ______________________________

Prayer Requests	Answers to Prayers
Week 1	
Week 2	
Week 3	
Week 4	
Week 5	
Week 6	
Week 7	
Week 8	

Week 9 (Long-Term Prayer Request)

"Pray for one another" James 5:16

PRAYER LOG

Name: ______________________________ Spouse: ______________________________

Cell Phone: ______________________________ Spouse Cell Phone: ______________________________

E-Mail Address: ______________________________ Spouse E-mail Address: ______________________________

Home Address: ______________________________ Children (ages): ______________________________

______________________________ ______________________________

______________________________ ______________________________

Home Phone: ______________________________ ______________________________

Prayer Requests	Answers to Prayers
Week 1	
Week 2	
Week 3	
Week 4	
Week 5	
Week 6	
Week 7	
Week 8	

Week 9 (Long-Term Prayer Request)

____

"Pray for one another" James 5:16

PRAYER LOG

Name: ______________________________

Cell Phone: ______________________________

E-Mail Address: ______________________________

Home Address: ______________________________

____

____

Home Phone: ______________________________

Spouse: ______________________________

Spouse Cell Phone: ______________________________

Spouse E-mail Address: ______________________________

Children (ages): ______________________________

____

____

____

Prayer Requests	Answers to Prayers
Week 1	
Week 2	
Week 3	
Week 4	
Week 5	
Week 6	
Week 7	
Week 8	

Week 9 (Long-Term Prayer Request)

____

"Pray for one another" James 5:16

PRAYER LOG

Name: ______________________ Spouse: ______________________

Cell Phone: ______________________ Spouse Cell Phone: ______________________

E-Mail Address: ______________________ Spouse E-mail Address: ______________________

Home Address: ______________________ Children (ages): ______________________

Home Phone: ______________________

Prayer Requests	Answers to Prayers
Week 1	
Week 2	
Week 3	
Week 4	
Week 5	
Week 6	
Week 7	
Week 8	

Week 9 (Long-Term Prayer Request)

"Pray for one another" James 5:16

PRAYER LOG

Name: ______________________ Spouse: ______________________
Cell Phone: ______________________ Spouse Cell Phone: ______________________
E-Mail Address: ______________________ Spouse E-mail Address: ______________________
Home Address: ______________________ Children (ages): ______________________

______________________ ______________________

______________________ ______________________

Home Phone: ______________________ ______________________

Prayer Requests	Answers to Prayers
Week 1	
Week 2	
Week 3	
Week 4	
Week 5	
Week 6	
Week 7	
Week 8	

Week 9 (Long-Term Prayer Request)

____

"Pray for one another" James 5:16

PRAYER LOG

Name: ______________________

Cell Phone: ______________________

E-Mail Address: ______________________

Home Address: ______________________

____

____

Home Phone: ______________________

Spouse: ______________________

Spouse Cell Phone: ______________________

Spouse E-mail Address: ______________________

Children (ages): ______________________

____

____

____

Prayer Requests	Answers to Prayers
Week 1	
Week 2	
Week 3	
Week 4	
Week 5	
Week 6	
Week 7	
Week 8	

Week 9 (Long-Term Prayer Request)

____

"Pray for one another" James 5:16

PRAYER LOG

Name: ______________________________

Cell Phone: ______________________________

E-Mail Address: ______________________________

Home Address: ______________________________

____

____

Home Phone: ______________________________

Spouse: ______________________________

Spouse Cell Phone: ______________________________

Spouse E-mail Address: ______________________________

Children (ages): ______________________________

____

____

____

Prayer Requests	Answers to Prayers
Week 1	
Week 2	
Week 3	
Week 4	
Week 5	
Week 6	
Week 7	
Week 8	

Week 9 (Long-Term Prayer Request)

____

"Pray for one another" James 5:16

PRAYER LOG

Name: ______________________

Cell Phone: ______________________

E-Mail Address: ______________________

Home Address: ______________________

____

____

Home Phone: ______________________

Spouse: ______________________

Spouse Cell Phone: ______________________

Spouse E-mail Address: ______________________

Children (ages): ______________________

____

____

____

Prayer Requests	Answers to Prayers
Week 1	
Week 2	
Week 3	
Week 4	
Week 5	
Week 6	
Week 7	
Week 8	

Week 9 (Long-Term Prayer Request)

____

"Pray for one another" James 5:16

PRAYER LOG

Name: ______________________________

Cell Phone: ______________________________

E-Mail Address: ______________________________

Home Address: ______________________________

____

____

Home Phone: ______________________________

Spouse: ______________________________

Spouse Cell Phone: ______________________________

Spouse E-mail Address: ______________________________

Children (ages): ______________________________

____

____

____

Prayer Requests	Answers to Prayers
Week 1	
Week 2	
Week 3	
Week 4	
Week 5	
Week 6	
Week 7	
Week 8	

Week 9 (Long-Term Prayer Request)

____

"Pray for one another" James 5:16

PRAYER LOG

Name: ______________________ Spouse: ______________________

Cell Phone: ______________________ Spouse Cell Phone: ______________________

E-Mail Address: ______________________ Spouse E-mail Address: ______________________

Home Address: ______________________ Children (ages): ______________________

Home Phone: ______________________

Prayer Requests	Answers to Prayers
Week 1	
Week 2	
Week 3	
Week 4	
Week 5	
Week 6	
Week 7	
Week 8	

Week 9 (Long-Term Prayer Request)

"Pray for one another" James 5:16

CARE LOG

Facilitators: ______________________________

Beginning Date of Study: ______________________________

PARTICIPANTS								
WEEK	INITIAL OF FACILITATOR RESPONSIBLE FOR CONTACT							
1								
2								
3								
4								
5								
6								
7								
8								
9								

DESCRIPTION OF SOCIAL ACTIVITY: ______________________________

CARE LOG

Facilitators: ______________________________

Beginning Date of Study: ______________________________

PARTICIPANTS								
WEEK	INITIAL OF FACILITATOR RESPONSIBLE FOR CONTACT							
1								
2								
3								
4								
5								
6								
7								
8								
9								

DESCRIPTION OF SOCIAL ACTIVITY: ______________________________

STUDY OBJECTIVES

1. Encourage people to experience a more intimate fellowship with Christ.

Luke 16:11 expresses the correlation between how we handle our resources and the quality of our fellowship with the Lord: *"Therefore if you have not been faithful in the use of worldly wealth, who will entrust the true riches to you?"*

2. Challenge the participants to invite Jesus Christ to be their Lord.

Money is a primary competitor with Christ for the lordship of our lives. Jesus said, *"No man can serve two masters, you will love one and hate the other... You cannot serve God and money"* (Matthew 6:24).

3. Teach participants God's way of handling money and motivate them to apply what they learn so that they can experience financial health.

4. Build close relationships among the participants.

FACILITATORS' RESPONSIBILITIES

1. Unconditionally love and encourage the participants. People are more receptive to spiritual truth when they have been loved. People want to know how much you care before they care how much you know.

2. Hold the participants accountable. This accountability will help the others in your group apply what they are learning so that their lives can be transformed for the better.

3. Be a model of faithfulness. Luke 6:40 reads, *"Everyone, after he has been fully trained, will be like his teacher."* Facilitators should be faithful to arrive early, pray consistently for the participants, know the memory verses fluently, and have their homework prepared.

4. Follow the Compass procedure of conducting the study. We've learned in thousands of small groups the most effective way to conduct this study, and your group will benefit doing it the proven way.

INFORMATION YOU NEED TO KNOW

1. **Facilitator's Guide.** The Facilitator's Guide is divided into (1) nine weekly sessions, (2) the prayer logs and care logs, and (3) the information facilitators need to know.

2. **Navigating Your Finances God's Way Video.** Each week toward the end of class you will play a segment of the *Navigating Your Finances God's Way DVD*. There are 9 segments of the DVD—one for each week of the study.

3. **Group Size.** It's best to limit the size to 12 including the facilitators, because the group dynamic is damaged if the group is too large. It's preferable for each group to have two facilitators in case one is unable to attend a meeting.

4. **Nine Weeks.** We strongly recommend that the groups meet once a week for the full nine weeks. However, it is optional to meet for fewer than nine weeks with the participants completing the remainder of the class by self-study.

5. **Meeting Time and Place.** The groups meet once a week for nine weeks. We strongly recommend that the classes be conducted in two hours, although it is possible to do it in less time if answers are abbreviated or groups are smaller. Groups may meet anywhere and anytime.

6. **Promoting Financial Products and Services.** No one may use their affiliation with Compass to promote or influence the sale of any investments or financial services or professional services.

7. **Tell Me About Compass.** Compass is an interdenominational ministry that trains people of all ages to apply the financial principles from the Bible. The reason it is named Compass is to remind us that we need God's financial direction. To learn more, visit www.compass1.org.

8. **Ordering Materials.** Materials may be ordered at www.compass1.org or by calling (407) 331-6000.

9. **Financial Information.** Compass—*finances God's way*™ is a non-profit, tax-exempt organization. The ministry is funded by course tuition and by tax-deductible donations, the bulk of which come from graduates of the study and churches Compass serves.

10. **Website.** Compass1.org is an excellent resource that contains many helpful tools, calculators, links to other websites and practical biblical financial teaching.

11. **Facilitator Training.** To learn more about becoming trained to be a facilitator of this study, visit www.compass1.org and click on "Small Group Studies."

ORIENTATION

As the group is being assembled, the facilitators should pray that the Lord will bring just the right couples into the group. Then the facilitators should meet with their group, about two weeks before the study begins, to hold an orientation. This may be done with just the members of your group, or it may be a church-wide or citywide orientation. At the orientation:

1. Begin to love the participants and build relationships.

2. Review the requirements.

The requirements are designed to take only about two hours each week outside of class. If someone comes to class unprepared, ask them not to participate in the discussion. The requirements are:

Daily homework
Scripture to memorize each week
Attend eight of the nine classes
Daily prayer for each participant
Weekly Let's Get Practical! exercise

3. Describe the other "ground rules"

Classes start and stop on time

Class opens and closes in prayer

Group discussions are confidential

Scriptures are memorized in the version used in the Compass materials

Participants are trained to be future facilitators by leading the weekly meetings.

No one will be embarrassed by being required to expose their financial situation

4. Dispense the materials and collect payment.

Each person enrolling in the study receives a manual. Collect payment for the class.

5. Assign the Week 1 homework.

The assignment for Week 1 is to read the book *Your Money Counts*, memorize Luke 16:11 and answer the homework questions. Ask everyone to bring their calendars to the first class to schedule the social.

6. Encourage all small group participants to register for the Compass e-newsletter.

Small group participants can log on to www.compass1.org and click on "Small Group Studies" to register for the free Compass e-newsletter and receive FREE and discounted resources.

PRAYER LOG

To help the participants develop a more consistent prayer life, we utilize the Prayer Logs starting on page 262. During the Week One meeting, ask each participant to provide the information at the top of the Prayer Log—their name, email address, etc.

- ☐ One Prayer Log should be filled out for each participant.
- ☐ End each class by taking prayer requests from each participant. The requests need not be limited to financial concerns. Prior to taking a request, inquire if they have experienced any answers to his or her previous requests.
- ☐ Ask the participants to complete their own Prayer Log before coming to class to save time. Each member prays daily for every member in the group during the nine weeks. Examine the sample Prayer Log below.

Name: Jim Dilworth
Spouse: Jennifer
Cell Phone: 555-312-6567
Spouse Cell Phone: 555-987-6543
E-Mail Address: jim@macl.com
Spouse E-mail Address: jend@wayoutl.net
Home Address: 272 Victor Ave.
Portland, ME 09445
Children (ages): Matt (11)
Danielle (5)
Home Phone: 555-1776

	Prayer Requests	Answers to Prayers
Week 1	MAtt recovers from illness Jim's relationship with boss improves	Matt feeling better
Week 2	Jim's relationship with boss improves friend comes to know Christ	

LOVING THE PARTICIPANTS

1. Love the participants inside of class

The facilitator's attitude should be loving, humble, and caring—not a critical or a "know-it-all" attitude. We are students among students, in that we all are growing in understanding the life-changing Word of God.

After a class member answers a question, encourage, affirm, and thank them. If an answer is incorrect, be careful not to discourage them by responding harshly or negatively. Maintain good eye contact, and be attentive. We communicate a great deal through our body language.

2. Love your students outside of class

Care log. The purpose of the Care Log is to ensure that the facilitators contact the members of their class each week to encourage and love them. The weekly contacts may be by telephone, mail, e-mail, text message or in person. The facilitators should alternate each week in making the contacts. The participants should not be aware of the Care Log.

CARE LOG

Facilitators: Ward and Mary Correll and Tim and Beth Diaz

Beginning Date of Study: March 9, 2011

		PARTICIPANTS						
WEEK	INITIAL OF FACILITATOR RESPONSIBLE FOR CONTACT	Taliyah Faith	Tim & Beth Diaz	Nancy Thomas	Jason Poland	Ward Cornell	Mike & Tabatha Menendaz	Dale & Yolanda White
1		WC LETTER	WC PHONE	WC TEXT	WC LETTER		WC PHONE	WC LUNCH
2		TD FACEBOOK	TD COFFEE	TD PHONE	TD TEXT	TD NOTE	TD PHONE	TD TEXT
3								
4								
5								
6								
7								
8								
9								

DESCRIPTION OF SOCIAL ACTIVITY: COVER DISH DINNER AT CORRELL'S

HOW TO CONDUCT THE STUDY

1. Open with prayer. We recommend that you pray on your knees to express humble dependence upon the Lord.

2. Individually recite the Scripture to Memorize.

3. Conduct the group discussion. The discussion proceeds as follows:

For example, the women might answer Day One, the men, Day Two, and so on. Read the assigned Scriptures for each day's homework before answering the questions. Ask a different person to begin answering each day's homework questions.

A participant should answer all the questions for a particular day's homework at one time. We've learned this is important to end on time.

If someone has thoroughly answered a question, the others need not repeat the same answers. Other participants should share new insights.

4. Complete the items in the Remaining Agenda.

5. Share prayer requests and write them in the Prayer Logs.

6. End in prayer.

NOTE: Small Group Dynamics

Wrong Method
In Diagram 1, the sole focus is on the facilitator, who does all the talking. The other participants are passive. This is not how Compass is designed.

Correct Method
Diagram 2 reflects a group interacting with one another, and a facilitator who guides the discussion, giving everyone the freedom to express their insights and questions.

SELECT & TRAIN FUTURE FACILITATORS

1. Set the Stage

During the Orientation, explain to the participants that you are training them to be facilitators. Whether they become one depends upon their faithfulness during the class and their desire to facilitate.

2. Give Participants the Opportunity to Facilitate

Facilitators should lead weeks one and two. Then other participants should lead weeks three - nine.

3. Select Facilitators

Select only those participants who are faithful during the study. Second Timothy 2:2 communicates the importance of selecting faithful people: *"And the things, which you heard from me, entrust to faithful men* [and women], *who will be able to teach others also."*

4. Invite Facilitators

Any potential facilitator should be approved by church leadership if the study is conducted within a church. Once approved, invite them to facilitate the study. If they agree they need to be trained.

5. Training

To become qualified to facilitate a small group, they should order and become familiar with the Facilitator's Guide, and log on to www.compass1.org and click on "On-Demand Training."

HOW TO BEGIN COMPASS IN THE CHURCH

1. Introduce Compass to the pastor/church leadership.

Meet with the pastor and church leadership to explain the study. To successfully implement the study in a church, it is essential to have the active support of the church leadership.

2. Select and train small group facilitators.

The number that will need to be trained is determined by the number of groups the church wants to begin.

3. Select the students for the initial group(s).

The major objectives of the initial groups are to multiply the number of people qualified to facilitate and to enable some of the church leadership to experience the study.

4. Choose the first church coordinator.

The church coordinator (usually a layperson) has the overall responsibility of implementing Compass in the church. This position requires a commitment of time and effort. The pastor should be involved in the selection process. The first person serving in this role is often gifted as an initiator and may wish to groom a successor.

5. When Compass is opened to the church.

Bathe every presentation in prayer, asking the Lord to motivate the participants He wants in the study.

Communicate the content and benefits of the study, and never use "hard sell" tactics. Describe the requirements and the need to invest two hours preparing each week outside of class.

Churches have used several methods to present the study: A Compass graduate's personal recommendation to a friend, the pastor's recommendation from the pulpit, an announcement in the church handout, and a live or video testimony of a graduate in front of a class or the entire church.

PLACES TO SERVE

If you have a desire to help others experience *Navigating Your Finances God's Way*, there are four places you can serve with Compass.

1. As a Facilitator

The heroes of Compass are the facilitators because the small group is an amazing environment for genuine life change to take place.

2. On the Church Team

If you want to impact your entire church, you may serve as the Church Coordinator or on the church team.

3. On the City Team

If you have a desire to influence your community, you may serve as a volunteer on your local Area Team. In order for Compass to have a broad impact on a larger city or populated area, it's necessary to have a full-time Executive Director and a functioning team of volunteers.

4. Beyond the City

You may have a "missionary spirit" and wish to help introduce Compass to other cities and even other countries. If you wish to serve your city, or even beyond your city, visit www.compass1.org.

THE NEXT STEP

What I need to do to begin my group:

My facilitator or co-facilitator is: ______________________________

My potential small group participants are:

______________________ ______________________

______________________ ______________________

______________________ ______________________

______________________ ______________________

Schedule the Orientation (location and date): ______________________________

____

My goal is to start my group by this date: ______________________________